2004 POE

ONCE UPON A RHYME

IMAGINATION FOR A NEW GENERATION

Kent Vol II
Edited by Steve Twelvetree

George
Page 40

Young Writers

First published in Great Britain in 2004 by:
Young Writers
Remus House
Coltsfoot Drive
Peterborough
PE2 9JX
Telephone: 01733 890066
Website: www.youngwriters.co.uk

All Rights Reserved

© Copyright Contributors 2004

SB ISBN 1 84460 539 6

Foreword

Young Writers was established in 1991 and has been passionately devoted to the promotion of reading and writing in children and young adults ever since. The quest continues today. Young Writers remains as committed to engendering the fostering of burgeoning poetic and literary talent as ever.

This year's Young Writers competition has proven as vibrant and dynamic as ever and we are delighted to present a showcase of the best poetry from across the UK. Each poem has been carefully selected from a wealth of *Once Upon A Rhyme* entries before ultimately being published in this, our twelfth primary school poetry series.

Once again, we have been supremely impressed by the overall high quality of the entries we have received. The imagination, energy and creativity which has gone into each young writer's entry made choosing the best poems a challenging and often difficult but ultimately hugely rewarding task - the general high standard of the work submitted amply vindicating this opportunity to bring their poetry to a larger appreciative audience.

We sincerely hope you are pleased with our final selection and that you will enjoy *Once Upon A Rhyme Kent Vol II* for many years to come.

Contents

Billie Kirby (10)	1
Stephen Munn (10)	1

Brenzett CE Primary School

Nadine Haydock (10)	2
Max Long (10)	2
Sianne Natt (11)	3
Bradley Clark (11)	3
Melanie Tardif (10)	4
Harry Garner (10)	4
Charlie Hoffman (10)	5
Abbie Laker (10)	5
George Wright (10)	5
Sonny-James Spencer (10)	6
Mathew Clark (11)	6
Amy Wooding (11)	7
Beth Wyatt (10)	7
Sophie Newman (10)	7
Ben Holt (10)	8
Zachary Holmes (11)	8
Thomas Baldock (10)	8
Samuel Rodgers (11)	9

Brookland CE Primary School

Aaron Leppard (10)	9
Bethany Dare (9)	10
Sophie Richardson (9)	10
Toby Roger (10)	11
Daniella Tosh (11)	11
Lily Hannon (10)	12
Bethany Bradford (10)	12
Stephen Shoebridge (10)	13
Aaron Gearing (9)	13
Laura Maidment (9)	14
Jack Chambers (9)	14
Jake Constable (10)	15

Days Lane Primary School

Billy Rigby (10)	15
Samantha Jarvis (8)	16
Jordan Hassan (9)	16
Isabelle Jones (8)	17
Duran Georgette (9)	17
Lucy Allen (9)	18
Adam Lenton (9)	18
Alan Jones (10)	19
Sophie Jones (9)	19
Amelia Hurley (9)	20
Michael Ryall (9)	20
Rhea Campbell (9)	21
Ashley Saunders (9)	21
Winnie Fee (10)	22
Eloise Baker (9)	22
Ashley Coward (9)	23
Jake Freestone (9)	23
Jake Featherstone (10)	24
Zainab Conteh & Rachel Ribbins (11)	24
Kirk Porter (9)	25
George Daws & Ben Cross (11)	25
Megan Wheatley (8)	26
Fred Kemp (9)	26
Emma Coyne (9)	27
Alfie Hughes (10)	27
Jordan Dunning (9)	28
Sarah Murray (8)	28
Jake Davies (10)	29
Emily Chandler (11)	29
Dale Traquair (10)	30
Billy Townsend (11)	30
Jodie Sewell (10)	31
Emily Fyfe (10)	31
Spencer Bush (10)	32
Robert Kent (9)	33
Scott Goodrich (10)	33
Nicholas Lott (11)	34
Frankie Thomas (9)	34
Nathan Berry (11)	35
Joseph Woodlands (10)	35

Rosemary Lewis (10)	36
Jason Donoghue (9)	36
Aidan Hallbell (11)	37
Michael Brough (10)	37
Sophie Dixon (9)	38
Sophie Taylor (9)	38
Grace Perry (8)	39
Luke Tapponnier (9)	39
Daniel Rouse (8)	40
George Wingfield (9)	40
Pippa Clark (9)	41
Emma Wilson (9)	41
Jack Newark (10)	42
Lauren O'Brien (10)	42
Joe Chaplin (10)	43
Elliott Hulf (9)	43
David Martin (10)	44
Mysah Muttur (9)	44
Jessica Miller (9)	45
Harrison Preston (9)	45
Laura Gearey (9)	46
Ceyhan Cemal (9)	46
Harry Baldock (9)	47
Jay Harrison-Smith (9)	47
Jacob Quieros (8)	48
Toby Crook-Haines (9)	48
Jake McGreig (9)	49
Emily Gurney (8)	49
Leigha Triance (10)	50
Tanyel Arif (9)	50
Holly Cook (8)	51
Amar Garcha (9)	51
Paige Curran (9)	52
Rachel Fuller (10)	52
Emma Winchester (9)	53
Stephanie Smith (9)	53
Ben Fuller (11)	54
Megan Johnson (9)	54
Kelly Lloyd (9)	55
Sian Duffy (10)	55
Jake Bryan (9)	56
Georgina Schwencke (10)	56

Nicola Wellings (9)	57
Lewis Pankhurst (10)	57
Brooke Clayton (11)	58
Nahid Wadud (9)	58
Bradley Pool (8)	59
Ben Lott (8)	59
Charlotte Stone (10)	60
Amy Oke (9)	60
Alex Hill (10)	61
Michael Hines (9)	61
Peter Douglas (8)	62
Lorna Johnson (8)	62
Emine Hassan (11)	63
Emily Jull (9)	63
Helen Paige (10)	64
Samantha Francis (9)	64
Matthew Langford (10)	65
Sam Woodcock (11)	65
Lauren Jacob (10)	66
Edward Keit (10)	66
Elizabeth Munday (8)	67
Joe Flanagan (11)	67
Matthew Callaghan (10)	68
Warren Strong (11)	69
Shannon Doyle (11)	70
Sam Thompson (11)	70
Charlotte Tremlett (10)	71
Roberto Faratro (10)	71
Jack Gregory (11)	72
Lauren Strong-Perrin (10)	72
Rachel Wilson (11)	73
Jade Bristow (11)	73
Natasha Ryland (11)	74
Richard Hill (10) & Aaron Gannon (11)	74
Amy Campbell (10)	75
Chloe Raggett (11)	75
Aron Rieger (10) & Nathan Bowman (11)	76
Daniel Furlonger (10)	76
Bret Stanley (10) & Tom Bassett (11)	77
Kay Clark (11)	77
Rhys Crane (10) & Eren Arif (11)	78
Rhian Whiting (10)	79

Gemma York (10)	79
Jack Cliburn (10)	80
Nicole Muskett (10)	80
Billy Holloway (11)	81
Lucan Pearce (10)	81
Shelly Parish (8)	82
Victoria Hobbs (10)	83
Nicholas Maslin (11)	84
Jamie Francis (10)	84
Danny Plummer (10)	85
Samuel Bowden (10)	85
Ellie Cruickshank (9)	86
Lauren Westpfel (11)	86
Matthew Brown (10)	87
Thomas Baynes (10)	87
Shannon Counsell (9)	88
Ellie Sparham (9)	88
Rachel Ellen Featherstone (8)	89
Katherine Pell (8)	89
Nese Louisa Redjep (10)	90
Sally Born (10)	90
Victoria Camfield (9)	91
Hannah Camfield (11)	91
Ben Quieros (9)	92
Terry Scott (10)	92
Matthew Dowdall (11)	93
Elliott Roberts (9)	93
Louise Kenney (9)	94
Sarah May Langford (9)	94
Harry Ervin (10)	95
Lucy Fawsitt (9)	95
Amy Elizabeth Moore (10)	96

Grove Park Community Primary School

Gemma Short (9)	96
Zara Wilkins (9)	97
Robyn-Marie Kenyon (7)	97
Summer-Paige Walsom (10)	97
Reece Michael Allen (8)	98
Beth Forecast (10)	98
Danielle Parry (7)	98

Robyn Cesary (11)	99
Rachel Foulger (10)	99
Charlotte Skinner (8)	100
Tiffany Sequeira (7)	100
Emma Ripley (11)	101
Ellena Hurst (9)	101
Nardiah Beasley (8)	102
Jamie Emmett (10)	102
Nicola Amy Cook (8)	102
Sammy Singleton (11)	103
Jessica Holmes (7)	103
Robert Maxted (11)	104
Samantha Daniels (8)	105
Lucy Katherine Horne (9)	105
Dean Rogers (7)	106
Vanessa McLane (7)	106

Ightham County Primary School

Bronwyn Shishkin (9)	106
Carys Herbert (7)	107
Shannon Thomas (9)	107
James Hayman (11)	108
Hattie Linley (7)	108
Hannah Hawkins (9)	109
Natalie Stroud (10)	109
Georgia Marsh	110
Owen Herbert (10)	111
Rosanna Cousins (10)	112
Ione Storey (10)	113

Murston County Junior School

Catherine Bevan (11)	113
Jessica Emptage (10)	114
Natasha Wimble (10)	115
Hayley Eve Elliott (10)	115
Chloe Smith (10)	116

Newington CE Primary School

Megan Locker (9)	116
Emma Jennings (9)	117
Daisy-Mae Cole (8)	117

Ellie Pinnock (8)   118
Michaela Louise Hearnden (8)   118
Natasha Clia Elliott (7)   119
Annabel Rose West (7)   119
Bronwen Mary Barton (8)   120

North Borough Junior School
Megan Rich (9)   120
Ben Smith (10)   121
Hannah Crickmore (9)   121
Ronnie Angel (9)   122
Tom East (9)   122
Claire Beevis (9)   123
Kirstie Humphrey (10)   123
Gemma Saunders (9)   124
Kara Emily Fox (9)   124
Katie Young (10)   125
Emma Bunch (10)   125
Liam Misson (9)   126
Saffron Ord (9)   126
Anna Stevens (9)   127
Francesca Evans (9)   127
Tim Thorne (9)   128
George Coster (10)   129
Jack Kiernan (10)   129
Isobel Emery (9)   130
Joe Hollamby (9)   130
Ryan Jeffreys (10)   131
Abby Winter (10)   131
Jayde Crittenden (9)   132
Abinash Joshi (9)   132
Zoe Butchers (10)   133
Sam Jeffs (9)   133
Liam Chapman (10)   134

Plaxtol CP School
Ursula Evans (9)   134
Christopher Bowles (10)   135
Alia Kassem (9)   135
Mattie Cracknell (10)   136
Reece Plummer (9)   136

Natasha Holberton (10)	137
Albert Chilman (10)	137
Olivia Betts (11)	138
Robyn Clarke (10)	138
Emily Crawford (11)	139
Elizabeth Pearce (9)	139
Jack Lusher (10)	140
Polly Coumbe (9)	140
Alice Pike (9)	140
Alex Bolam (10)	141
Michael Woodgate (11)	141
Nicolle Aiston (10)	142

St James' RC Primary School, Petts Wood

Robert Adams (11)	142
Ellen Costello (11)	143
Nicholas Greenwood (10)	143
Luke Brook (11)	144
Ronan Napier (10)	144
John Hatch (10)	144
Lucy Pereira (11)	145
Hannah Williams (11)	145
Alice Ballard (10)	146
Rachel Allen (10)	146
Charles Turner (10)	146
Katrina Longhurst (11)	147
Joelle O'Neill (10)	147
Grace McCarthy (10)	147
Catherine Dow (11)	148
Jack Harper (10)	148
Josh Hughes (10)	149
Charlotte Weeks (10)	149

St John's CE Primary School, Maidstone

Jordan Blackwell (9)	150
Hannah Bailey (9)	150
Alexander Roy Milne (9)	151
Kasey Bryen (9)	151
Christopher Bennett (9)	152
Nicola Frost (10)	152
Andrew Mark Tingey (10)	153

Nicholas Li (9) 153
Adam O'Connell (10) 154
Danielle Barrington (10) 154
Emma-Jane Taylor (9) 155
Sarah Pole (10) 155
Deborah Batchelor (10) 156
Chandni Patel (9) 157
Michael Kitchin (9) 158
Ashley Usoh (9) 158
Maria Miles (10) 159
Emily Bown (10) 159
Chloe Swan (9) 160
Rhianna Eves (9) 160

St Peter's RC Primary School, Sittingbourne

Finn Collins (8) 160
Jack Harding (8) 161
Nicole Boakye (7) 161
Lewis Atkins (7) 161
Ellie Haddock (7) 162
Poppi-Anna Marie Conway (8) 162
Lauren Etherington (8) 162
Zoe Amy Thomas (7) 163
Eleanor Page (8) 163
Catherine Meiklejohn (7) 163
Beth Tumber (7) 164
Chloe Escritt (8) 164
Robert Gibson (9) 164
Jane Hammond (10) 165
Joshua Wells (10) 165
Siân Bradley (10) 165
Charlie Sewell (9) 166
Laura Cox (10) 166
Callum Molyneaux (9) 166
Louise Kahira (9) 167
Felícia Lane (9) 167
Sean Maher (10) 167
Deanna Ward (10) 168
Larrissa Way (9) 168
Emily Robertson (10) 169
Alice Lawson (9) 169

Marika Paslow (10)   170
Kelly Wratten (10)   170
Victoria Ward (9)   170
Miles Hutchinson (10)   171
Emilia Sage (10)   171
George Butcher (9)   171
Charlie Heathfield (9)   172

Seal CE Primary School
Emily Burston (9)   172
Amy Primett (8)   172
Hannah Lowe (8)   173
Sophie Obbard (7)   173
Oliver Maxwell (7)   173
Kirby Sammonds (8)   174
James Coppins (8)   174
Michael McGinniss (7)   174
Dylan Evans (7)   175
Cy Gadd (7)   175
Iestyn Gadd (7)   175

South Borough Primary School
Jack Treeby (11)   176
Daniel Baines (10)   176
Kirsty Ross (10)   177
Nicola Johnston (10)   177
Tasha Atkinson (10)   178
Laura Walker (10)   179
Emily Smith (10)   180
Joanna Dillon (10)   180
Erin Anne Ross Elmer (9)   181
Philip Ellwood (11)   181
Jamie Potten (10)   182
Ellie Stevens (8)   182
Rosie McGinn (10)   183
Adam Ross (8)   183
Giorgia Daniels (10)   184
Hibah Zubair (7)   184
Rebecca Smy (10)   185
Hannah Reilly (9)   185
Ellie King (8)   186

Leon Alcock (10)	186
Emma Whyatt (10)	187
Dean Wilson (10)	187
Kirsty Samson (7)	188
Jessica McCafferty (10)	189
Bethany Taylor (7)	189

Wentworth Primary School

Ashleigh Maria Haines (10)	189
Brandon Lee (10)	190
Ben Crome (10)	190
Olivia Dove (9)	191
Samantha Perry (11)	191
Nicola Thomas (10)	192
Abi Tait (11)	192
Kerry Mills (11)	193
Elen Harris (11)	193
Alice Palmer (10)	194
Paul Moran (11)	195
Michelle Martin (10)	196
Ben Hodges (11)	197
Katherine Joyce (11)	198
Sean Middlemiss (10)	198
Hayley Newman (11)	199
Billy Cox (11)	199

The Poems

Bluebird

Once I met a bluebird
His name was Postbird Pat,
He flew in the sky over houses
Wearing a postbird hat.

One day he was posting letters
Fell in the big post box,
It was dark and really scary
And he was sure he saw a fox.

The bad news was he really did
So bluebird tried to get out,
Fox bit off bluebird's tail
So bluebird started to shout.

But the good news was he did get out
And ran away home,
He was so, so scared that he shivered
And was glad he was all alone.

Billie Kirby (10)

Hullabaloo!

T heme parks are so fun,
H owling and screaming,
E ven if you're moving,
M oving cups go round,
E ven when your heart is pounding.

P leading, so desperate,
A sking to go on,
R oller coasters go streaming by,
K een to go on.

Stephen Munn (10)

The Sun

Saw the sun rise in the morning,
Rising, glowing in the morning,
Saw the brightness steaming from it,
Whispered, 'What is that, Grandfather?'
And the good grandfather answered:
'Tis the fire of the great God,
Fire of the god of lightning,
Argued with the god of darkness,
Argued all day and all the night,
For who to rule, the dark or light?
Will light rule or will the dark fall?
Mighty Zeus came and said to them,
Said to share or he'll come again,
Came again and told a message,
Light half the day, dark the other,
Darkness no more in the daytime,
In the day sunshine shines only,
So that's how the sun came to be.'

Nadine Haydock (10)
Brenzett CE Primary School

A Description Of Chris

Spiky black hair running past you,
Looking like a big black
Fur ball flying past you,
Eyes like a big blue waterfall,
Always trying to MC in a calm voice,
You can talk to him like a good friend,
He always smells of Lynx deodorant,
Always wearing nice clothes on non-uniform day,
He is a very good friend you can hang around with.

Max Long (10)
Brenzett CE Primary School

Why It Frosts

Saw the frost on silver branches,
Silver sparkling frosted branches,
Saw the spider's web a-sparkling,
Whispered, 'What is that, grandfather?'
And his good grandfather answered,
'Once a young Snow Queen was arguing,
Arguing with the rising, red sun,
They argued till day turned to night,
That night the Snow Queen got angry,
Angry with shining, hot sun,
Angry that every time she went near,
Him she started to melt away,
She decided to cast a spell,
A crafty spell that would change night-time,
Every night it shall sprinkle with frost,
Covering the world like sparkling glitter,
Till the rising sun awakes,
So the Snow Queen ruled night-time
And the sun ruled daytime,
Then from that fine magical night,
Neither the sun or Snow Queen
Had reason to argue again.'

Sianne Natt (11)
Brenzett CE Primary School

Pigeon

A pigeon flies in the ocean blue sky,
It never wastes time in the sky,
A pigeon's wings are the power of the sky,
The pigeon's soul flies with the wind.

Bradley Clark (11)
Brenzett CE Primary School

Autumn Leaves

Saw leaves of autumn change colour,
Burning brilliant red-brown colour,
Saw the sparkling leaves a-glowing,
Whispered, 'Why is that grandfather?'
And the old grandfather answered:
'You know the powerful God Coal,
He needed a world of colour,
So changed the sea to royal blue,
So changed the tree trunks to beauty brown,
Red, he wanted the leaves to be,
Had no red, his colour ran low,
For only one season the red would glow,
Leaves became the colour of green,
One season a year the red would glow,
Gorgeous green for the rest of the year.'

Melanie Tardif (10)
Brenzett CE Primary School

My Best Friend

My best friend, Bradley Clark
He is a kind and helpful boy
He always wants to help
He is a smart and clever boy
He has spiky-up hair
And is a great pigeon lover
My best friend, Bradley Clark
He has brown sparkly eyes
He is a small boy
Although he's small, he's still tough
He always has his collar up
And hardly gets his work wrong
My best friend, Bradley Clark.

Harry Garner (10)
Brenzett CE Primary School

The Arsenal Ground

The green shiny grass
Like the blade of a sword
The lines marked plain white
Fans cramming through the gates
Not a single space
Out come the Arsenal squad
The fans all go mad
Arsenal, Arsenal.

Charlie Hoffman (10)
Brenzett CE Primary School

My Nephew, Harry

I have a nephew called Harry
He has ginger hair
He's always crying and laughing
And always pulling my hair
He's always playing and singing
Having too much fun
Always wearing smart clothes
Sometimes wearing none!

Abbie Laker (10)
Brenzett CE Primary School

My Holiday In New Zealand

See mountains with fluffy Christmas snow on the top,
People snapping their cameras,
Water rippling from the ice,
Loud noisy helicopters flying past,
Hearing people loudly laughing.

George Wright (10)
Brenzett CE Primary School

My Sister Issy,

My sister, Issy
Makes me dizzy,
Watching her spin round,
She's sometimes annoying,
But never boring,
She's sometimes bad
And sometimes glad
And normally very mad,
When it comes to school,
She never plays the fool,
She really thinks she is so cool,
Teacher's pet,
That's what I bet!

Sonny-James Spencer (10)
Brenzett CE Primary School

Things That Make Me Happy

Crashing roller coaster
Chatty people
Clashing, splashing water
Burgers smelling
Hot, exciting
A brilliant holiday!

Curly grey hair
Eyes that make me feel warm
A voice like gentle hay
Helps to do things
Smells of expensive perfume
A lovely nan!

Mathew Clark (11)
Brenzett CE Primary School

My Grandad

My grandad has grey, feathery, sticky-out hair,
His big round eyes are like two gleaming crystals,
When we see him, he always says, 'How's she cutting?'
He does good impressions and always teases me,
He is warm and soft and has a faint smell of smoke,
He usually wears a T-shirt and black trousers,
He is the best grandad on Earth.

Amy Wooding (11)
Brenzett CE Primary School

My Sister

She always argues with me
And never likes the cup of tea
I make her
She smells of strawberries
And sometimes gives me cuddles
I miss her when she goes out
She's my big sister.

Beth Wyatt (10)
Brenzett CE Primary School

My Sister

Lopping brown hair over her eyes like curly waves,
Eyes as clear as the blue sky,
Calling, 'Let's play again,' in a childish voice,
Her scent like flowers growing in a garden,
Casual clothes like T-shirt and dungarees,
Her smile lights me up,
She trusts me and believes in me.

Sophie Newman (10)
Brenzett CE Primary School

My Dog, Lucy

My dog is called Lucy,
She's a bit goosy,
She's got big brown eyes,
They're as big as the skies,
She's black not blue,
But she still gets the blues,
When she's in the cellar,
She acts like a fella,
When she sleeps,
She sleeps in peace.

Ben Holt (10)
Brenzett CE Primary School

Winter

Frozen tears silently still
Sick people still taking pills
Ice soundlessly melting
Snowballs are still flying
A new year begins.

Zachary Holmes (11)
Brenzett CE Primary School

Heaven

In the heavens up above
In the rainbow of good souls
You shall find a calming sea
Like a summer's lovely day
You shall find your own good love
You will see it in your son.

Thomas Baldock (10)
Brenzett CE Primary School

Autumn Leaves

Saw the autumn leaves change colour
Fantastic flaming red-brown colour
Whispered, 'Why is that, Grandfather?'
And the good grandfather answered.

'Many moons ago there were two gods,
Zuke and Zelda were these two gods,
They argued till day turned to night,
About which colour leaves were right.

Should they be green or maybe brown?
Zuke liked them green but Zelda, brown,
Leaves would change colour all day long
But neither god thought he was wrong.

One day Zuke said it had to end,
These arguments they had to end,
No changing colour brown to green,
The same hue for months should be seen.

Ever since then leaves start off green,
Spring and summer colour then seen.
But autumn colour turns to brown
And stays with us till all fall down.'

Samuel Rodgers (11)
Brenzett CE Primary School

The Cheetah

She is a fit, healthy girl.
She is a flash of lightning.
She is the open land runner in the day.
She is a friendly animal and very sensitive.
She is as black as the dark, dark night
And as yellow as the bright sun.

Aaron Leppard (10)
Brookland CE Primary School

The Ferrari Of The Jungle

The Ferrari of the jungle is as
fast as a human going down a slide

He lies deep in thought alone but aware

His long silky tail stroking the branch

Its spotty skin as furry as a freshly sheared sheep

Its pointed ears and anxious eyes
Stare below the tall tree

He lies in wonder looking for prey

His eyebrows droop as he lies in suspension

He slides down the tree and creeps
Along the crusty leaves.

Then he pounces and tucks
Into a big chunk of meat.

Bethany Dare (9)
Brookland CE Primary School

Guess Who?

He is a hairy, tall, wide, chubby man
Sitting deep in thought.

He is a strong tree covered with leaves
Darting from forest to forest.

He is a deep, dark jungle
Waiting for light to come.

He is a sad antique from
Antiques Roadshow.

He is as black as a black hole
From mysterious space.

What is he thinking?
What is he doing?
How long will it take us to find out?

Sophie Richardson (9)
Brookland CE Primary School

The Terminator

The almighty one, the stomping bulldozer, making its way
Through the broad savannah
Turning the landscape baron

The earth shakes, the sky above rumbles like thunder and lightning,
Leaving the others confused, wondering what on earth is going on.

The empty bewildered eyes stare,
Like traffic lights stopping and staring,
He rolls in the river, crushing the vegetation with his shoulder pads.

The trumpet blows, time to run, clear the area
A stampede is on its way,
Destroying everything in its path like a hurricane causing chaos
In a city with herds of people panicking, lost in confusion.

The giant finally comes to rest,
Its rubbery rough skin as grey as a rain-filled cloud,
Daydreaming with a mind of its own.

Toby Roger (10)
Brookland CE Primary School

The House Pet

She is one of the favourite cuddly, loving house pets,
She hops around exploring her furnished surrounding,
She has big, bold, blue eyes so she can spy its predator
                                                    coming nearer,
She can live out in the wild but she can also live in a clean cage,
She can be all different sizes, large or small and all different
                                                    shapes, fat or thin,
She can run as fast as the wind when trying to get away
                                                    from its predator,
She can be all different colours such as grey, black, white and brown,
She can identify when human footsteps or the predator's
                                                    footsteps are coming,
She can live in dark, gloomy forests or in brown, clean cages,
Can you guess what my animal is?

Daniella Tosh (11)
Brookland CE Primary School

The Sharp Blade

The sharp blade looked forward,
While he was burning bright,
He looked very vicious,
Like he was going to get me.

I looked at the burning colour
And his sharp eyes
And then he moved his paw forward
And stared in my eyes.

If I moved away from him,
He would prance forward,
Who knew what his claws behold,
Maybe just a scratch or two?

The burning light is getting closer,
What am I meant to do?
First I'll step,
Then I'll run!

Lily Hannon (10)
Brookland CE Primary School

The Play Toy

The playful house pet, the boss of the house has awoken.
A sweet, crawling baby, soft and warm,
Exploring down below, level with long, spindly table legs.
He is raring to go, happy
And searching for tasty tit-bits.
Golden as the ever-shining sun,
Its rays wandering off to lost places.
He can hear sounds in the forbidden upper world,
What is up there?
He won't venture that far.
He settles down once more,
Only to awake when the raindrops tiptoe on the roof.

Bethany Bradford (10)
Brookland CE Primary School

Pollution

Pollution is a grey gust of
smoke filling the air.
Pollution is because of toxic waste
and that is not fair.

Pollution is a crumbled building
destroying the land.
Pollution is a black slimy sea
crashing over the sand.

Pollution is loose oil,
creating black slime.
Pollution is near,
we haven't got much time.

Pollution is putting your
rubbish in the bin.
You do not know you
are doing a sin.

Pollution is near,
pollution is coming,
it soon will be here.

Stephen Shoebridge (10)
Brookland CE Primary School

The Basilisk

The skinny Basilisk has a long roped tail
Which can wipe creatures in its way
This lonely creature lives in the dull
Old river with lots of fish
Its skinny legs skip across the long running river
His colour is a greeny-grey with a scaly tail and body
This skinny Basilisk croaks at night
And he lives on insects and fish.

Aaron Gearing (9)
Brookland CE Primary School

The White Ball Of Fluff

The small tiny fluff of white fur
Like a man wrapping his own child
In a warm bundle of white cotton

The white ball of wool is like you can't see it in the snow
Its claws and teeth are like a brand new knife

The white ball of fur lives far out in the cold
Where the freezing icebergs float out to sea

The white ball of snow catches fish like a shark
Is quick at its prey, its mood so calm
And gentle and sometime its anger is like a volcano
About to erupt

The white ball is as white as a snowflake
Just fallen from the sky
So bitter with a chill of coldness.

Laura Maidment (9)
Brookland CE Primary School

The Athlete Of The Prairie

The athlete of the prairie was warming up for his busy day ahead.
If you heard it, you would think there was a siren right behind you.
He had already begun to plan his sabotage on the other athletes
To make sure he would win.
As the race began, the chase was on
And his plan began to take place.
He passed some athletes who he knew wouldn't even reach halfway.
More perished prey began to fall back,
Giving the athlete more and more food
And more and more energy.
The water pistol filled with toxins didn't need to reload
But it kept squirting out his opponents
As if a massive water fight had broken out
When the athlete had reached the finish line with a full stomach
He knew not even one of the other athletes
Would ever reach the end.

Jack Chambers (9)
Brookland CE Primary School

Waiting!

It sits on the shallow water waiting,
Waiting for its prey,
Its scaly skin rubbing the deep ocean water.

It has teeth as sharp as a razorblade
And jaws as powerful as a crane.

It lays waiting for the prey to come a little bit closer
Before it pounces at it.

Jaws wide open, it launches itself at the fish,
Jaws clutched around its fins.

Blood oozing out of it.

The fish try to swim away
But was dragged down into the reeds.

It is as green as a tropical rainforest,
With bark for its eyes,
Its scales are as thick as a tree's trunk.

It plans its vicious attack meticulously,
Waiting for a bigger bite, waiting for you.

Jake Constable (10)
Brookland CE Primary School

Homework Excuses

'My big dog tore it to bits'
'I will let you off today'

'A big gorilla pulled it out of my hand'
'That's OK I understand'

'A big flying phoenix burnt it to bits'
'I did not know that phoenixes existed'

'A big flying UFO zapped it away'
'Do you expect me to believe that today?'

Billy Rigby (10)
Days Lane Primary School

Apostrophe Poem

Best remembered:
My nan's flat,
My sister's sun hat,
My aunty's house,
My cousin's mouse,
My sister's fish,
My mum's wish.

Best forgotten:
My dog's sharp bite,
My sister's broken kite,
My nan's burglary,
My sister's scared face,
My grandad's false teeth,
My cat's sharp claws.

Samantha Jarvis (8)
Days Lane Primary School

Apostrophe Poem

Best remembered:
My brother's PS2.
My mum's smelly perfume.
My grandad's big belly.
My brother's boring video.
My rhino's roaring.
My dad's white dressing gown.
My mum's big blue car.
My big white guitar.
My grandad's strong appetite.
My nan's big glasses.

Best forgotten:
My brother's PS1.
My mum's pink pyjamas.
My uncle's wink.

Jordan Hassan (9)
Days Lane Primary School

Apostrophe Poem

Best remembered:
My cat's soft fur,
My mum's big hugs,
My sister's Disney mugs,
My dog's happy face,
My best friend's smiles

Best forgotten:
My cat's sharp long claws,
My dog's big paws,
My mum's smelly feet,
My sister's short fringe,
My grandma's annoying whinge,
My niece's screaming cry.

Isabelle Jones (8)
Days Lane Primary School

Apostrophe Poem

Best remembered:
My mummy's cuddles,
My daddy's giggles,
My giraffe standing in London Zoo,
Looking at my brother's smiles,
Looking at my friend's smile,
My brother's aftershave,
My best friend's cats.

Best forgotten:
My dad's ice cream,
My dad's aftershave,
My dad's hairy beard,
My dad's smoking,
My brother's scooter.

Duran Georgette (9)
Days Lane Primary School

Apostrophe Poem

Best remembered:
My niece's curly hair,
My nephew's little bear,
My chocolate's creamy middle,
I love my sister's giggle,
My mum's arm around me,
My friends hurting their knees,
My friend's scary stories.

Best forgotten:
My sisters being bossy,
My friend's flossy hair,
My horrible days,
My friend's ways,
My dad's chocolate's middle,
My friend's silly giggle,
My best friend's other best friend.

Lucy Allen (9)
Days Lane Primary School

Food!

Food, food, we chomp and chew,
Food, food, we munch and crunch,
Sausages are scrumptious, chips are munchious,
Mash, mash, I dash just to get at it!
Never eat greens they make you weak
Sponge is great, especially with custard,
Hot dogs as well with mustard!

Food, food, we chomp and chew,
Food, food, we munch and crunch!
Nuggets are great with a shake,
Ice cream as well, it's swell,
Cake's great, it draws me like bait!
So you know what to do . . .
Eat food!

Adam Lenton (9)
Days Lane Primary School

He Who Never Walks

I am he who never walks
He who never talks
Only he who flows

My whirlpool teeth shall swallow you whole
People cry in my sight as I hit them

I can get through any hole
I am all around you
There is no escape from the almighty sea

I can sink cities
I can grab you from the shore
And I'm sure you'll never be seen again

I am never calm, always mad
I don't care about you, just me!

Alan Jones (10)
Days Lane Primary School

What Is Life?

What is life?
Why are we here?
How do we think and remember things?
Why are we here? Do you know?

How does the sun send
Light and heat?
How does the rain come down
And cool you in the blaze?

Who do you know who was here at the beginning,
Beginning, beginning?
And who will be here at the end of the Earth?
So much to find out,
I wish I knew it all.

Sophie Jones (9)
Days Lane Primary School

Love Poem!

My lips are as red as roses
My eyes are as blue as the sea

I feel like I'm going to burst
My heart's pounding with love

I stroll against sunset trying to find love
I only hope God is watching from above

I'm sitting alone by the fire at night
Feeling warm and fuzzy about the one I love

I wear a golden silk dress with diamonds dotted all around it
My shoes are made out of diamonds too

If I go away the sun will go in
There will be a big storm
And everyone will be unhappy
When I'm here the sun smiles and shines happily away
And everyone is really happy!

I walk by the beach one night
I see a man, is it love at first sight?
No it isn't!
I still sit alone by the fire at night
Feeling warm and fuzzy
But no one comes.

Amelia Hurley (9)
Days Lane Primary School

Birthday Candles

I make people happy by making myself sad,
When I'm shrinking all the time it doesn't make me glad!
People eat what I sit on and gobble it right down,
They all blow and spit on me, I don't agree at all,
People have a disco, they dance all through the night,
I like quite parties not a rabble in sight,
Their mouths we open, they look hungry,
It's time to put out my light!

Michael Ryall (9)
Days Lane Primary School

The Haunted Mansion

Dilapidated mansion
With a small window at the very top
Open the creaky door
It sounds like a warning
Very unwelcoming

The curving grand stairs
Go on and on and on!
Trees tremble, children scream as they peer in,
But no one enters!

The cupboards open and shut themselves,
Laughing and laughing.
A roaring fire in the rusty grate,
Cobwebs in the corners watching your every move,
Spiders crawling up the walls
And on your hands and legs!

Rhea Campbell (9)
Days Lane Primary School

The Dragon's Lair

My breath is like a firework getting set off
My lair is like a dark, damp swamp
I think everybody that comes to my lair has a bad feeling

So when people come to my lair I pretend I am asleep
When they come in and I breathe fire
People get scared and try to run away

My mouth is as wide as a gate
I am as strong as a volcano's lava
I am as scary as a dilapidated mansion

People run when they see me
My lair is like a volcano eruption
People try to sneak in but don't succeed

I am as fast as the speed of light
My lair is as dark as night-time.

Ashley Saunders (9)
Days Lane Primary School

I Am An Angel

As I spread light from Heaven which leads to the door of dreams!
My white dress, as smooth as silk,
Sways from side to side,
As my wings flutter through the space around me.

My halo glows when the moon comes out,
Like sparkling butterflies in the peaceful air,
The clouds fall from the sky as I step on them one by one,
The clouds turned into pixie dust like a fairy has granted a wish!

As I hang the stars up at night,
I place the moon in the middle,
Then watch the children rest,
Looking down under.

Then I enter the golden gate of Heaven,
Sometimes I rest my eyes gently on the comfy pillow
And say a prayer before my sweet dreams.

Winnie Fee (10)
Days Lane Primary School

Little Brothers

L ittle brothers, little sisters
I have one, do you?
T heir toddling never ends
T hey're taking everything in sight
L urking round the corners
E avesdroppers is what they're going to become

B ig brothers, big sisters
R adios on extremely loud
O bserving everything
T alking to their friends and
H urriedly going to nights out
E ating party food
R abble here, rabble there, so there are
S isters, brothers everywhere, life isn't such a nightmare.

Eloise Baker (9)
Days Lane Primary School

The Haunting House!

As I tiptoe around haunting the road at night,
I hear owls howling, people screaming and shouting,
My heart pounds like I have been running for one hour,
As I approach number 16, only 3 more houses till I reach it!
The trees look like I have done something wrong,
As I step nearer the door there is a sign
It says *Beware Of This House!*

As I open the door slowly it starts to creak,
The whole door slams behind me
And it sounds like a bomb exploding.

When I step into the living room
It sounds like there is a bunch of ghosts in the house,
As I go upstairs roof tiles crack
And it sounds like ice is beaming!

Just when I step into the haunted bedroom
I hear someone open the door,
I run downstairs,
The old lady walks into the living room
And I finally get out!

Ashley Coward (9)
Days Lane Primary School

The Last Candle On The Shelf

I'm the last one on the shelf
There's no one here except me
This upsets me
I'm an ugly colour and a bad smell
I'm so far back on the empty shelf
Finally someone buys me
But then puts me away forever.

Jake Freestone (9)
Days Lane Primary School

Fire!

I am as hot as an oven
I am as destructive as a meteor
I laugh as I destroy the Earth
And I snigger as you make your pitiful attempts to stop me!

I can sweep fields
And from outer space you can see my screaming face
You cry as your homes die
As I come towards you, you see my mad face, you freeze in fright!

No one can destroy me!
As I dry up your brainless rivers
And I toast your forests for lunch!
I kick the Earth with my burning feet!

You beg for rain,
You want winter,
Your wishes come true,
My enemy comes,
I die, but you know I'm going to return!

Jake Featherstone (10)
Days Lane Primary School

Polar Bears

Polar bears are big and strong,
Like a queen, they eat all day long.
As lofty as a large snowball,
Ears like tiny spheres of cotton wool.

Bodies as great as an igloo,
Giant velvet paws like soft dough,
Gullible like human beings,
The bravest of them all.

Polar bears as clean as a sheet,
Noses like buttons on a shirt.
As tough as leather in their skin,
Their long, sharp teeth like icicles.

Zainab Conteh & Rachel Ribbins (11)
Days Lane Primary School

I Wish

I wish I was a bird in the morning sky
Swishing swirling up and down
Like a swan in the sunset swimming shallow
And as beautiful as a dove carrying the carriage
Of Aphrodite softly in the sky

I wish I was a tiger prowling in the jungle
Pouncing and killing its prey

I wish I was a kangaroo
Because its legs are trampolines
Falling free in the air

I wish I was a cheetah
As fast as the wind
I can just imagine it the fast, cold wind flapping
On my face like a hairdryer on full blast.

Kirk Porter (9)
Days Lane Primary School

David Beckham

He's the golden boots of football,
He's as cool as a cucumber,
He can get the ball over the wall,
Corners, penalties and free kicks,
This is what he does best out of the picks.

He's as fast as a cheetah,
He can run so far,
His best footballer friend Is Lua Lua,
His different hairstyles are like a pony,
Don't get me wrong his hair is not phoney.

He's the England captain,
But he is still thin,
He never loses, he always wins,
He left Manchester for Madrid,
He now plays centre mid.

George Daws & Ben Cross (11)
Days Lane Primary School

Swimming

Swimming, swimming
It's a wonderful sport
I really ought to go
A bit more`

It's not a bore
You have to be
As strong as Thor
To swim 6 lengths

My mum says
That I'm as powerful
As a hound swimming
But not running on the ground

I can dive down, down, down
And don't drown, drown, drown.

Now I go swimming more
And I'm as strong as Thor.

Megan Wheatley (8)
Days Lane Primary School

DJ Decks

DJ decks
DJ decks
I like you
DJ mix them
You twist them
You fix them
Booming, banging
Crashing and bashing
You mix them
You twist them
You fix them
You beat them.

Fred Kemp (9)
Days Lane Primary School

Instruments

Orchestra today time to play,
I can't wait to go to school today
Because we've got so many exciting things to do
I'm walking to school today
With my mum to get a bit of fresh air

So when I got to school
I kissed my mum goodbye
And went into the room
Where we have a lesson
I play the violin and my friends play the chimes
We learnt how to play
'Joe-Joe stumped his toe'
And had a chat about going to the rat hall
To play our instruments and sing some songs
Our lesson is finished now
And I have learnt a lot today
It's time to say bye-bye
So bye-bye then.

Emma Coyne (9)
Days Lane Primary School

Roller Coaster

Higher and higher I climb to the sky
Fear in my face, tear in my eye
I swoop down with a speed of fright
The wind whizzing by like a sky-high kite
When I get off, the fear has gone

I get one more, it goes higher than I have ever gone
Down it crashes to the ground
Round and round, up and down
As it rapidly goes along the track.

Alfie Hughes (10)
Days Lane Primary School

Animals

Why aren't I a cheetah
As fast as the
Wind?
Why aren't I?

Why aren't I a fox
As sly
As my little
Brother?

Why aren't I a monkey
As bendy
As plastic?

Why aren't I
As fierce
As a T-rex?

Jordan Dunning (9)
Days Lane Primary School

Best Remembered!

My dog's teeth
They gnaw through beef

My kitten's feet
They look so neat

My monkey's loud burp
My hippo's big slurp

My budgie's feathers
My kitten's a treasure

My frog's big splash
My toad loves potato mash

My bunny's big hop
My horse's loud clop.

Sarah Murray (8)
Days Lane Primary School

Foxes

Foxes, foxes,
Big or small,
Wide or thin,
Short or tall.

Foxes' fur
Is like a blur,
With the speed of light,
As fast as a kite.

Its eyes are beaming,
With its feet steaming,
Tail like a brush,
Like a squirrel in a rush.

Foxes, foxes,
Big or small,
Wide or thin,
Short or tall.

Jake Davies (10)
Days Lane Primary School

Treasure

Treasure is silver
Treasure is gold
Treasure stands out whether you're young or old

It's as pretty as a rainbow
As bold as the sea
Treasure is spectacular when you give it to me

Treasure is a necklace
Treasure is a ring
Treasure is a wonderful, beautiful thing.

Emily Chandler (11)
Days Lane Primary School

Speed Control

Screeching off the starting line, going twenty miles an hour,
Reaching nought to sixty and using all the power,
All of the racers have a need for speed,
Racing around the corner and taking the lead,
If your car is rusty when the sign says go,
Don't bother racing if your car is slow.

Nitrous bursts like a lion's roar,
They race around a circuit, it's not against the law,
Every classic car has multicoloured paint,
If your engine blows there's no complaint,
Your car is stylish if you've got nineteen inch rims,
The sound system pumping, it will tear your limbs,
You have top of the range interior and quick gear shift,
You go too wide, you've done a good drift.

Dale Traquair (10)
Days Lane Primary School

A Spell For Romance

A bunch of flowers, a kiss to you,
Waiting in Heaven a rose or two,
A box of chocolates, a wing of a dove,
This will bring out true love.

We mix this for a romantic spell,
This love we give you may never tell.

I have tried and tried to get into your heart,
Now we may never be apart,
Take her to dinner, you will be the winner,
Give her a kiss, can you do all this?

We mix this for a romantic spell,
This love we give you may never tell.

Billy Townsend (11)
Days Lane Primary School

The Snow

The snow springing quietly on top of my house
Is a white rabbit as small as a cat's paw
Dropping its food with such a small clatter
Which isn't a very big matter

The snow blobbing on top of my house
Is little foam balls as small as a mouse
Hanging about in places I do not want
But I have no choice but to have it on top of my house

The snow scuttling round my house
Is little white ants as small as lice turning to ice
Whirling around like no one cares
Snow!

Jodie Sewell (10)
Days Lane Primary School

A Poem Of Love

Wool of a sheep, mixed with sweets
Magic from a wand, fish from a pond
Pixies' feet and a loved one's treat
Tail of a monkey to make it funky

Fairies' toes, petals from a rose
Dust from a star, a golden bar
Witches' sparkle, little rascal
Angels' wing, children sing

Silver glitter, lemons bitter
A bird's feathers and cow's leather
Black cat, tail of a rat
Paw of a kitten, a baby's mitten

Stir this well to make your loved one fun.

Emily Fyfe (10)
Days Lane Primary School

Animals

Think of a bee,
as large as a tree.
Think of a bat,
as fat as a cat.

Think of a dog,
as big as a hog.
Think of a frog,
as small as a Pog.

Think of a snake,
as thin as a rake.
Think of a bear,
as sweet as a pear.

Think of a slug,
as hard as a thug.
Think of a snail,
as big as a whale.

Think of a tiger,
as small as a spider.
Think of an eel,
as fat as a seal.

Think of a bug,
as flat as a rug.
Think of me,
as fat as can be.

Spencer Bush (10)
Days Lane Primary School

Apostrophe Poem

Best possessions:
My dad's nice shoes,
My mum's new shirt,
My brother's nice football,
My sister's new skirt,
My kitten's cute face,
My friend's nice bike

Worst possessions:
My brother's good reflexes,
My other brother's biting,
My head teacher's hair,
My cat's smelly food,
My brother's boring books,
My other brother's boring game.

Robert Kent (9)
Days Lane Primary School

Snake

He sways from side to side
Glaring all around
Never misses his target
And always makes a sound

His pattern's like a tiger's stripes
Tail is a sharp pin
He hisses and rattles
And has harsh skin.

Scott Goodrich (10)
Days Lane Primary School

Blue

The river water is blue, deep and warm,
Swim carefully through it.

The chameleon is blue, spiky and rough
When he is by the river.

The sky is blue, a blinding blue,
When it rains big, heavy raindrops.

Jeans are blue, leather and smooth,
Mum wears them every day.

The water is blue, tasty and cold,
In the summer it's nice to gulp.

The ink is blue, creamy and dribbly,
It doesn't smell nice, but looks brilliant.

Tears are blue, sour and pretty,
They drip down your face when you are sad.

Nicholas Lott (11)
Days Lane Primary School

The Lion

He snakes through vines for his prey
Zoom! He jumps rapidly to protect his family
His eyes like black spheres
As strong as an ox
As elegant as a crane
With fluffy yellow fur, with a bright orange mane

The lion stalks his prey and waits for the right moment
He pounces for his food
His mind is set on his prey
For the sake of his survival, food is needed
He knows killing is wrong
But the sake of his children, he must kill!

Frankie Thomas (9)
Days Lane Primary School

Cool Animals

Cats are as pretty as a flower,
sometimes they have lots of power.
Dogs are as loud as a foghorn,
they might be quieter when they're born.
Rabbits are fluffy balls,
they always eat vegetable pools.
Horses are as bold as brass,
they also eat lots of grass.
Hippos are as heavy as rocks,
for them it's fast when they see their clocks.
Birds fly as high as planes,
you see lots on wide plains.
Grasshoppers are as green as grass,
one time I saw one in my class.
Penguins are as black and white as an old movie,
the way they walk is weird and groovy.
Monkeys are as brown as a box
and almost as sly as a small fox.
Parrots are as colourful as a pencil case,
by the way, never challenge them to a race.

Nathan Berry (11)
Days Lane Primary School

Football

Football is a vicious war between two teams
Football is god to its supporters
It makes me cheer when a goal goes in
Whenever there is a corner I always think of cornflakes
When there is a goal kick it makes me want to take the mick
Whenever there is a penalty
There is a strange mentality
Whenever there is a free kick
I think of my uncle Rick.

Joseph Woodlands (10)
Days Lane Primary School

Fruit

Oranges glow like the sun,
But kiwis are as brown as mud.
Bananas like a crescent moon,
Strawberries are as red as blood.

I like juicy succulent peaches,
Plums are like the sky at sunset.
Ripe nectarines are golden beaches,
Mangos like the jungle floor.

Grapes are sitting on the vine,
Cherries are like glowing rubies.
Grapes waiting to be crushed to wine,
Melons like golden footballs.

Pineapples' leaves are like the thorns on a rose,
Apples gleam in the sun.
Coconuts fall down as the wind blows,
Best of all, apricots taste like gold.

Rosemary Lewis (10)
Days Lane Primary School

The Beach

Sand as white as snow
But as hot as lava
Palm trees flapping like a bird
In the hectic wind
People running across the ocean floor
And crashing into the warm water
Crabs scampering across the Pacific
Boats in the distance away from shore
The hot sun belting down on the sunbathers
Melting away their cream
The volleyball players hitting the ball
Covering the sun
Time to go home, see you next summer.

Jason Donoghue (9)
Days Lane Primary School

My Dog

My dog is like lightning
And hates sightseeing.
He never calms down
And never shows a frown.

My dog is like a guard,
He never lets us down.
We always give him a treat,
He's definitely neat.

My dog is like a boss,
He gets whatever he wants.
We take him out twice a day,
Three times if it's May.

He eats like a lion,
His food is mostly meat.
He speeds to his food,
On his little padded feet.

Aidan Hallbell (11)
Days Lane Primary School

Snakessssss

Slithering through the damp green grass
Night or day they are ready to strike with their poisoned fangs
As blind as a bat, their forked-shaped tongue senses their prey
And kills it and swallows it whole
And slithering to find food to eat again till they're full
So beware
Some can be
Slow
Some can be fast
Some can go under
Some can be as dangerous, as dangerous as can be
Some are disguised
Some are nocturnal
Snakes have a popularity of thousands.

Michael Brough (10)
Days Lane Primary School

Snow

The snow drizzles down
Not making a sound
It's as white as white paper
Then it goes but it comes back later
I throw a snowball at my sister
And it gives her an enormous blister
I build a snowman
As quickly as I possibly can

As I play out in the fluffy snow
I run as fast as I can go
Wait! The snow's coming down faster
And my sister comes out with a plaster
I run through the crunchy, icy snow
And I trip over and hurt my toe

So then I come out with a plaster
Oh isn't that a disaster
The next day I look out of my window, while I get dressed
And the snow has gone, only slush is left.

Sophie Dixon (9)
Days Lane Primary School

My Pet Cat

My pet cat is ginger and white,
Pads along in the deep dark night.
Creeps around quiet as can be
And goes asleep away from the family.

Her name is Honey,
She plays with her ball,
She likes her bed
And comes when I call.

Sophie Taylor (9)
Days Lane Primary School

Best Remembered

My dog's flapping ears
have been flapping for years

My grandad's look of love
he would of loved to see a dove

My best friend's smile
looks like a crocodile

My brother's suit
he plays the flute

My dog's food
she's in a bad mood

My grandad's smelly socks
and his noses is always blocked

My friend's cup of tea
she ate a frozen pea

My brother's scruffy room
he always needs a broom.

Grace Perry (8)
Days Lane Primary School

The Rattlesnake

Slithering through
The long green grass
The rattlesnake
Moves like a
Sock full of jelly
His tough scaly skin
Bumping, sliding through the ground
He slops and hides
Laying silently, watching
Waiting for its dinner!

Luke Tapponnier (9)
Days Lane Primary School

Apostrophe Poem

Best remembered:
My brother's old trainers,
My dog's big floppy ears,
My gran's Sunday roast,
My mum's excellent telly programmes,
My dad's fun games,
My nan's soft voice,
My rabbit's big teeth,
My grandfather's loud laughter,
My uncle's old car.

Best forgotten:
My grandmother's boring games,
My dog's long claws,
My great nan's loud voice,
My rabbit's fluffy fur,
My cat's boring purr,
My nan's boring telly programmes,
My brother's boring picture,
My snail's small shell,
My auntie's old house.

Daniel Rouse (8)
Days Lane Primary School

Dragon

He's as big as 20 towers
He swoops down as swiftly as a leaf
Eyes as sharp as an eagle
He silently flies over the misty mountains
He breathes fire that would melt all the metal in seconds
If you even touched his horns your hand would be in shreds
This bloodthirsty monster
Would eat you at first sight.

George Wingfield (9)
Days Lane Primary School

Snow

The icy, slushy snow diving down
Children making a snowman
Cars slipping on black ice
The older children playing snowball fights
The snowflakes like tiny diamonds and pearls
Falling on the rooftops
Rivers turned to ice
Everybody wet and soggy

The snow is still falling by my house
Like an iceberg slamming on the window
Me and my brother rush outside
Playing snowball fights
While Mother is still inside

But now it's summer
I can rest in my paddling pool!

Pippa Clark (9)
Days Lane Primary School

My Cat

A cat playing happily
Miaow! Miaow! Miaow!
Its eyes are like small black balls
Fur as soft as candyfloss
And a lovely grey colour
Ears are pointing up like rooftops
Paws as small as a mouse

She jumps up at her toy mouse
Her jump is as high as a giant
And her paws get higher than ever
Suddenly she curls up in a ball
And goes to sleep . . .

Emma Wilson (9)
Days Lane Primary School

Football Frenzy

There was a man called Dave
Who played for London Town
He took a dopey free-kick
And missed an open goal

The next day he was better
Much better than before
But he still missed a penalty
And tripped over the ball

The next day he met Beckham
Who trained him very hard
Free-kicks are now his speciality
And curling corners far

The last game of the season
He was the best of all
He scored from a free kick
And got appreciated by the manager of Cornwall!

Jack Newark (10)
Days Lane Primary School

The Alien From The Spaceship

As he plods along
Looking around
I see him coming into the ground
Everyone stares at his big bold eyes
Nobody knows where he comes from
Someone goes and tries to fight
Panting and puffing with all their might
All the alien's green, fat, slimy body
Crinkles and wrinkles as he gets angry
Everyone gasps as the boy takes his shot and
Smack an arrow hits the alien in the back
He waddles back to his spaceship
In a big grey hat
People have a party, but will he come back?

Lauren O'Brien (10)
Days Lane Primary School

The Dog

The dog marched down the street
Like a king
His eyes like golf balls!
His tail like a shoelace
He was the king of the street!
He lives in a palace
That's what he thinks . . .

His name was King Rhoma, last name Charlie
He is the king of dogs
He was the king of beauty
He lives in a house near a fire

But one day he went out to play
Everyone was horrible to him
He went back in his house
He was hungry but the owners were not in
So he got his dog biscuits.

Joe Chaplin (10)
Days Lane Primary School

Football Freddy

There's a boy called Fred
Who liked to sleep in his bed
When he woke up
His dad said, 'Man U won the cup'

The next day Fred went out to play
And he missed an open goal that day
So he went home
And he gave a moan

The next day he came out
And he ran all about
He found a ball
And had a fall
And never came out again.

Elliott Hulf (9)
Days Lane Primary School

The Fire Dragon

He flies as quick as lightning
His fire as hot as a furnace
The dragon lives in darkness
The dragon's wings are like thick leather
He shoots across the misty wasteland
He has horns as sharp as spikes

The dragon is feared by all
He's as tall as a tower
He hovers like a bag in an updraft
The bloodthirsty creature is as vile as a hyena
This vile creature hunts in the pitch-black night
It's as fierce as a lion
But it lives for a long 20,000 years.

David Martin (10)
Days Lane Primary School

Elephant's Look

E lephants as grey as fog,
L ots of tusks as white as snow,
E xtra big feet, round as round as can be,
P ainless trunks as deadly as poison,
H airless relative to the mammoth,
A s big as giants,
N ever ever forgetting, for elephants never forget,
T ough as a rhino,
S afari jungles are their homes.

L oud and bold they are the leaders,
O ther animals burn with envy,
O utstanding elephants,
K iller animals come for a match but always fail.

Mysah Muttur (9)
Days Lane Primary School

Chestnut Horse

A horse steadily galloped through a long green field
Zoom! Neigh!
Teeth as sparkly as a disco ball
Hooves as heavy as metal
Eyes as big as golf balls
Mane as bushy as a lion

He jumped *crash!*
He fell and tried again
Whizz!
Jumped it
Oh yes!
Off he galloped to another jump

Yes, he got over it
What a wonderful jump
Cantering back to the stable
He had a gulp of water
A lonely rest was needed after a stressful day.

Jessica Miller (9)
Days Lane Primary School

The Snake

As the slippery snake slithers through the grass,
As it eats its prey.
The snake's patterns
Glitter in the darkness
And it rustles over the ground,
It slithers in the swamp,
With a hiss here
And rattle there,
Nobody dares to enter his territory.

Harrison Preston (9)
Days Lane Primary School

Me And My Mum

Best remembered:
Me and my mum's wonderful song,
We love to play ping-pong.
My mum's pink flower,
My banana was sour.
My bright yellow hat,
My mum's green mat.

Best forgotten:
For my mum's tea,
I gave her a green pea.
Laura's pink boots,
My mum's huge green book.
After lunch,
I had a crunch.
I was sad,
My mum was mad.
All my toys
Make a noise.
My mum's smile
Is like a crocodile.

Laura Gearey (9)
Days Lane Primary School

Crocodile Crunch

The crocodile cuts through the water
Looking for his prey
He swags his tail slower than a snail
He tries to find his way
His teeth as hard as metal
His tail as long as a snake
He gets faster and faster as he spots his target in the lake
He gets closer and closer and then . . .
Munch! Crunch! He's eaten the whole bunch.

Ceyhan Cemal (9)
Days Lane Primary School

Apostrophe Poem

Best possessions:
My PS2's games,
My ball's bounce,
My robot dog's movement,
My baseball bat's ball,
My metal detector's finding,
My dad's car,
My bed's cover,
My PC's internet,
My bike's speed.

Worst possessions:
My dog's bad smell,
My uncle's dog's bite,
My clock's alarm,
My mum's hard brick,
My mum's car,
My friend's water bombs,
My book's small words
My sister's lying.

Harry Baldock (9)
Days Lane Primary School

Apostrophe Poem

My dog's white bone sits in a throne
My sister's cat likes eating bats
My best friend's cow swims with a whale
My dad's clock wears one sock
My mum's funfair looks like a polar bear
My brother's car likes going to the bar
My nan's window likes playing bingo
My cat's paw opened the door
My best friend's sink likes to wink
My neighbour's wig looks like a pig.

Jay Harrison-Smith (9)
Days Lane Primary School

Apostrophe Poem

Best remembered:
My friend's house
Is as quiet as a mouse.
My sister's rabbit
Is her habit.
My neighbour's dog
Sits on a log.
My cat's purr
Shivers his fur.
My nan's cat
Wears a big black hat.
My dad's gold ring
Gets chucked in the bin

Best forgotten:
My friend's shoes
Always loose.
My mum's green peas
Go in her tea.
My dad's hairy beard
Turns him weird.
Jacob aged eight
Has a super mate.

Jacob Quieros (8)
Days Lane Primary School

Apostrophe Poem

My best friend's dog likes to play in the fog
My best friend's dog likes a particular frog
My best friend's lips love to suck chips
My best friend's hat looks like a huge cat
My sister's fox likes to play in a box
My dog's paw is so very sore.

Toby Crook-Haines (9)
Days Lane Primary School

Apostrophe Poem

Best remembered:
My brother's sneaks
He likes hide-and-seek
My dad's laugh
He takes the short path
My mum's job
She likes corn on the cob
My grandad's garage
He got some badges
My family's large frog
Likes jumping on logs
My brother's lonely fish
Likes to go splish
My nan's recipe
Is nice enough for me
My neighbour's house is bold
It is going to be sold.

Jake McGreig (9)
Days Lane Primary School

An Apostrophe Poem

My dad's black hat,
My best friend's ginger cat,
My sister's teddy bear,
My mum's fair hair,
My brother's stripy suit,
My nan's green newt,
My grandad's old clocks,
My cousin's smelly socks,
My auntie's fierce dog,
A farmer's snorting hog,
My dad's sore head,
My mum's new bed.

Emily Gurney (8)
Days Lane Primary School

Scales On A Fish

Scales on a fish,
One of them is me,
I like being a scale,
It makes me feel pretty,
But I feel sorry for humans because
They don't have scales
That glisten like sparkly socks.

I like being a scale,
Because everyone can see,
How beautiful I am and everyone
Wishes that they had me,
I'm so lush and so lean,
I sparkle like a smile,
But not one that's mean.

Leigha Triance (10)
Days Lane Primary School

Best Remembered

My dog's fairest fur,
Reminds me of my cat's pearl,
M77y hamster's teeth,
My dog's beef,
My friend's hair
Is as cuddly as a bear,
My dolphin's fins
Flap like wings,
My fish's eyes
Like the sight of pies,
My secret box
Has a very powerful lock,
My budgie's feathers
Looks like leather.

Tanyel Arif (9)
Days Lane Primary School

Best Remembered

Best remembered:
My dog's sharp teeth
Gnaw through juicy beef,
My dad's prickly beard
People say he's weird,
My sister's hair
So beautiful and fair,
My mum's smile
Runs for a mile,
My brother's toys
Always make a noise,
My neighbour's cat
Likes to eat rats.

Best forgotten:
My dad's hairy legs,
My mum's washing pegs,
My sister's knotty hair,
My dog's cuddly bear,
My friend's fluffy poodle,
My neighbour's disgusting noodles.

Holly Cook (8)
Days Lane Primary School

The School Test

As I'm about to do my test
The teacher says, 'Do your best.'
The first question was 7+7
So I wrote 77
The second question was 11+11
So I put my hand up, 'Can I have the answers?'
'No!' shouted Miss Glancers
2 days later I got my paper
Out of 10 my score was 7!

Amar Garcha (9)
Days Lane Primary School

My Dog, Morty

Strong as an ox
Brave as a bear
He goes through life
Without a care

He's got a tail
But it's so small
You would think
He would have
No tail at all

He's got a coat
Sleek and fine
His big brown eyes
Look into mine

What is he thinking of?
Bones or a walk?
What would he say
If he could talk?

Paige Curran (9)
Days Lane Primary School

Santa Claus

S tockings hanging by the fire
A ll the girls and boys in bed
N o presents if you stay awake
T onight is the night
A ngels sweetly sing

C hristmas time has come again
L eave out brandy for Santa
A nd a carrot for Rudolph
U p in the sky
S anta says bye-bye.

Rachel Fuller (10)
Days Lane Primary School

Dolphins

I love dolphins
They're the best
The way they twirl
And never stop to rest

I love dolphins
They're so sweet
They are very
Nice to meet

I love dolphins
The way they glide
Alongside boats
They seem full of pride

I love dolphins
They're so pretty
Very cunning
And also witty!

Emma Winchester (9)
Days Lane Primary School

The Sun

The sun is the one
Who shines down on the Earth

The sun is the one
Who helps flowers give birth

The sun is the one
Who gives us light

But the moon is the one
Who shines down on us
During the night.

Stephanie Smith (9)
Days Lane Primary School

Chocolate

Chocolate is as soft as a teddy,
Ding, the chocolate is now ready,
Chocolate is a statue,
Which you mould into shape.

Chocolate is a lemon,
Bursting with flavoured melon.
Chocolate is a lump of wood,
I've cut out of a forest.

Chocolate is as yummy as a roasted chicken
And is good for licking.
Chocolate is a hungry horse,
Galloping around your mouth.

Chocolate is as cheeky as a monkey
And it looks really funky.
Chocolate is as brown as wet soil
And I like to share it with my neighbour.

Ben Fuller (11)
Days Lane Primary School

Rufus, Rufus

Rufus, Rufus jolly goofus,
You jump on my bed,
You jump on my head,
But as long as you're there
I don't really care
Loofus, goofus, I love you Rufus
So why don't you chase me some more?
I hope you're around for a long time
And I'm glad you'll always be mine.

Megan Johnson (9)
Days Lane Primary School

My Family

Best remembered:
My sister's curly hair
My friend's laugh
My mum's coat
My dad's car
My nan's glasses
My grandad's football
My hamster's wheel

Best forgotten:
My sister's scream
My friend's howling
My mum's loud voice
My dad's phone
My nan's moan
My grandad's hiss
My hamster's missed.

Kelly Lloyd (9)
Days Lane Primary School

Black And White Panda

Slow strides through the trees
Nibbling on bamboo
Swing through the trees
Gently as can be
But you will not like
To cuddle one for you will get a fright
For it will grab you
And scratch

With eyes like black shiny pearls
With fur like candyfloss
And fur black and white
As snow and coal.

Sian Duffy (10)
Days Lane Primary School

Best Remembered

Best remembered:
My golf team,
My brother's PlayStation,
My little brother's toys,
My dad's snoring,
My glasses,
My grandad's laughter,
My nan's house.

Best not remembered:
My cousin's football team, Millwall
My brother's Game Boy,
My old glasses,
My old toys,
My mum's cooking,
My nan's football,
My grandad's football team, Chelsea.

Jake Bryan (9)
Days Lane Primary School

The Puma

The hunting puma bites through his food
It pulls its prey into caves and trees
Away from all the other predators
He stores up all his catches
To feed his starving family

He strides back to his home
With the leftovers in his mouth

As soon as he is back
He lies quietly on the floor
For a good night's sleep
And in the morning
He will hunt for his family again.

Georgina Schwencke (10)
Days Lane Primary School

Best Remembered

Best remembered:
My cat's quiet purr.
My fish's clean tank.
My mum's pretty smile.
My dad's big hugs.
My sister's straight hair.
My best friend's happy laugh.
My grandad's good stories.

Best forgotten:
My cat's sharp teeth.
My fish's wide mouth.
My mum's hard smacks.
My dad's loud singing.
My sister's horrid arguments.
My best friend's nasty looks.
My grandad's tight hugs.

Nicola Wellings (9)
Days Lane Primary School

Football

Football crazy, football mad,
West Ham came to the Lions' ground
Millwall have a shot
We get on the spot
Oh, what a spinning shot!
West Ham too had a sporty shot
But oh yes! They missed the spot

Oh, we don't get a shock
When we go to the clock
Oh, but West Ham are not
Worth a grand
Oh, but Millwall are just
The best of all.

Lewis Pankhurst (10)
Days Lane Primary School

School Today

Today we had a supply teacher,
She was the backbone of our school.

Her eyes were like shiny sapphires,
She was as busy as a bee.

She was as fat as a tree trunk,
When she walked through doors.

She had to be as cool as a cucumber,
Because of the boys.

She was as funny as a cat
On a mat eating spaghetti.

She was like a bulldozer in the school
Because of all the children.

When it was time for her to leave,
We hoped we'd see her soon.

Brooke Clayton (11)
Days Lane Primary School

Dark Shadow

The dark shadow has a miserable smile,
He is black and quiet and scary,
But no one dares to take him to trial
And he obviously scared the father of Queen Mary.

The dark shadow is as black as burnt wood,
Will never show his real view,
He hides his head in a dark hood,
Will kill anything that is blue.

The shadow is long and freaky,
Creeps behind and kills,
Probably kills people mostly,
Wouldn't care if the victim is bigger than 1,000 hills.

Nahid Wadud (9)
Days Lane Primary School

Best Remembered

Best remembered:
The dog's cold water,
The bird's yummy food,
The grandad's fake teeth,
The old lady's nice tablets,
The child's fun football,
The rat's long tail,
The dad's fast car.

Best forgotten:
The dog's sloppy mouth,
The bird's white poos,
The grandad's blurry glasses,
The old lady's walking stick,
The child's loud voice,
The rat's smelly cheese,
The dad's boring jokes.

Bradley Pool (8)
Days Lane Primary School

Best Remembered

Best remembered:
My hamster's smile,
My cat's dark eyes,
My brother's Xbox,
My football team,
My car's colour,
My mum's friend.

Best forgotten:
My hamster's bite,
My cat's scratch,
My school's homework,
My sister's moan,
My teddy bear's clothes,
My wellington boots.

Ben Lott (8)
Days Lane Primary School

Mad House

I live in a mad house
And this is how it goes,
My dad is a footballer
And he twists, spins and gives us a pose,
He says he is as cool as a cucumber,
But that's another lie.

My mum is the cook
And loves to cook pie,
Her eyes are rubies, diamonds
And sapphires, well that's what we say,
Mad house, mad house, mad house.

My sister loves to go to school
And play in our swimming pool,
She says the water is the sky
And the people swimming
Are the bright, shining stars.

We have two silver cars,
One big, one small.

They have a horn that is as loud
As a football crowd when they score,
Mad house, mad house, mad house.

Charlotte Stone (10)
Days Lane Primary School

Winter

The winter's frosty ice,
The winter's crispy snow,
The winter's chilly wind,
In and out your legs it goes,
Running through your fingers,
Down your neck, up your shirt,
So wrap up warm,
Or you will freeze.

Amy Oke (9)
Days Lane Primary School

The Man From Nottingham

There once was a man from Nottingham,
Who tried to cross the river,
Look at the dope,
He tripped on a rope,
Now look at him shiver.

He begged for mercy like he was going to die,
He always was a stupid guy.
His servant was blind as a bat
And as foolish as a rat,
Now look at him shiver.

He got beaten by a hog
And ran like a dog
Because he was wet as lake,
Now look at him shiver.

It was his own fault
Because he tripped on a rope.
Look at the dope,
It was his own fault,
Now look at him shiver.

Alex Hill (10)
Days Lane Primary School

Imagination World

Badger in the bush,
Rustle in the tree,
Out pops a fox,
With the best of glee.
It has love,
It has power,
Then comes a rabbit
With a flower.

Michael Hines (9)
Days Lane Primary School

Jungle Poem

Sharks crunch
Tigers munch

Lions pounce
Kangaroos bounce

Snakes slide
Hawks glide

Crocodiles snap
Pythons wrap

Monkeys climb
Birds eat lime

Dolphins jump
Elephants thump

Cheetahs run
Cats are fun

Piranhas bite
Eagles fly like a kite

Tarantulas crawl
Buffalos rule the jungle

Bees sting
Sloths cling.

Peter Douglas (8)
Days Lane Primary School

My Life

My mum and dad as nice as could be
My sister is a terror just like me!
I have three goldfish as shiny as ever
And they mostly like the rainy weather!

Lorna Johnson (8)
Days Lane Primary School

The Sky

The sky is bright blue,
As blue as a sapphire.
The sky is up high,
High in the sky.

Clouds in the sky,
White puffs in the sky,
All different sizes.

Clouds in the sky are as beautiful
As a swan on the lake,
The sky is as different as Earth,
That is a big circular,
Circles the Earth,
Clouds are the fog,
They go everywhere like a frog,
Which I like the most!

Emine Hassan (11)
Days Lane Primary School

Underwater

John Dorie's dash
Seals splash,
Octopuses wriggle,
Clownfish giggle,
Sea turtles relax
Seaweed cracks
Swordfish fight
Piranhas bite
Dolphins jump
Pufferfish pump
Sea horses ride
Rays glide.

Emily Jull (9)
Days Lane Primary School

A Fruity Poem

Oranges are as round as the sun,
I always share them with my mum.
Nectarines taste like gold,
They never have any mould.

Strawberries are as red as a rose,
I always eat loads and loads.
Grapes are as green as grass,
They taste much better than Mars bars.

Apples are like winning footballs
And they taste like expensive jewels.
Cherries are as small as marbles,
They are also a bit like bubbles.

Melons are like big rugby balls,
They always find them on fruit and veg stalls.
Pineapples are like huge palm trees,
The top part of it is the leaves.

Helen Paige (10)
Days Lane Primary School

Animals

Elephants stamp
Tigers camp
Crocodiles crunch
Alligators munch
Snakes slide
Cheetahs hide
Hyenas giggle
Caterpillars wriggle.

Samantha Francis (9)
Days Lane Primary School

Father Christmas

Father Christmas' beard is white as snow
And I like the sound of him going ho ho ho.

His reindeer I thought they were hogs
And they are as brown as logs.

He is as shiny as a light
And he gives me a big fright.

The fire is glowing like a glow insect
And my brother acts like a prefect.

He gives me presents as big as a house
And last year he gave my sister a pet mouse.

But!

I love Christmas, it's so fun
Because there's treats for everyone.

Matthew Langford (10)
Days Lane Primary School

My Cousin

My cousin is as mad as a hatter,
All she does all day is chatter,
She dances and sings,
She thinks she has wings,
My cousin is as mad as a hatter.

My cousin is as pretty as a princess,
But all she does is make lots of mess,
She jumps around like a swimming owl
And knocks her juice down her shiny pink dress,
My cousin is as pretty as a princess.

My cousin is as silly as a clown,
She thinks she is rich,
But I think she is a meany old witch,
My cousin is as silly as a clown.

Sam Woodcock (11)
Days Lane Primary School

Blue

Blue is the colour
Of the sky
Without a cloud
Cool, bright and proud
Blue is the calm sea
The colour of ink
An ice rink
Blue is shadows on the snow
A feeling way down low
A sapphire ring
A lonely thing

Blue is the colour
Of children's shoes
With coloured laces
And swimming pools
Red, pink and blue wools
Blue is the colour of my dad's tools.

Lauren Jacob (10)
Days Lane Primary School

PlayStation

PlayStation is as black as a panther,
Its screen is a rainbow of colours
Its games are as a rainbow of colours
Its black sides are stripy as a black striped zebra
Black is like a burnt turkey
Black is on the side of your shoes
Black is darkness
Black clouds are forced towards lighting
Black in the moon
Black is the darkest stripe I've ever seen.

Edward Keit (10)
Days Lane Primary School

Best Remembered

Best remembered:
The dog's cute face
My sister's cheeky way
My dad's smile
My mum's kindness
My nan's cleverness
My grandad's silliness
My godmother's artistic way

Best forgotten:
The dog's growl
My sister's arguments
My dad's loud voice
My mum's hard nails
My nan's eyes
My grandad's tummy
My godmother's boys.

Elizabeth Munday (8)
Days Lane Primary School

My Pet Hamster

He has a white coat,
He eats like a goat.

He is very funky,
He is a cheeky monkey.

He has a tiny face,
He has a place in the hamster race.

He hides his food,
He is very rude.

He eats everything
And you can hear him sing.

He acts like a little superstar
Because he is my pet hamster.

Joe Flanagan (11)
Days Lane Primary School

A Poem To Chocolate

My favourite chocolate is as brown as a tree trunk,
It's so good that I gave it to a monk.
The chocolate of the world tastes like gold,
You can see it from anywhere it's so, so bold,
Expensive chocolate is as decorative as a picture,
I like it more than (and this is saying something) literature . . .

Milk chocolate, white chocolate,
Dark chocolate, chocolaty chocolate,
Chocolate with little toffee pieces,
Coffee chocolate, Belgian chocolate,
Swiss chocolate, Cadbury's chocolate
And chocolate with a truffle filling,
Nestlé chocolate, crunchy chocolate . . .
And don't forget Aero-o-o-s.

Chocolate can be as creamy as your skin,
It can be delicate, it can be very thin.
On the other hand, it can be as rough as the waves,
It really can save, save, save!
Melted chocolate is as runny as the sea,
This is just between you and me.

The chocolate has gone, the sun has died,
Now it's time to say goodbye.

Matthew Callaghan (10)
Days Lane Primary School

My Best Friend

My best friend is taller than a tree,
He smells like tea
And is ugly as can be.

His head is a melon,
He's always tellin'.
He is my best friend,
But he drives me round the bend.

His hair is orange,
Just like a carrot.
He is a parrot,
Always repeating himself.

He's never in with the latest trend,
He is a way good friend.

When he's going to tell,
He's like a bell.
He is a great big ape,
With every video tape.

If offered he will always take,
His eyes are as blue as a lake.

His nose
Is as long as a hose.
He's so weird,
He's grown a beard.

Warren Strong (11)
Days Lane Primary School

Red!

Red is the sunset that always fills the sky,
Red is the blood when it comes outside,
Red is the colour of a car that goes very fast,
Red as a rose on Valentine's, I like it the most when they are all mine,
Red is a bubbly fizz that is red and pink too.

Red is a ruby, they are very precious stones,
As red as the blood, a very angry thing,
The Devil is as red as a carpet just been bought.

Red is a juicy fruit,
They're nice and sweet and so watery too.
Red is something very strong,
Tastes like wine and gives you a kick.
Red is the colour of our literacy book
And it rhymes like the story of Captain Hook.

Shannon Doyle (11)
Days Lane Primary School

The Top Three

Arsenal are as red as a rose,
Whatever Wenger says goes.
Arsenal are known as the Gunners, when they're on the up,
They could of won the Carling Cup.

Man U are as evil as the Devil,
Especially Gary Neville.
The Devils are as big as a tower,
With a lot of power.

Chelsea are as blue as the sea,
Roman Ambromovich is as busy as a bee.
Chelsea are as rich as the Queen,
Only when she's keen.

Sam Thompson (11)
Days Lane Primary School

White

As white as a feathered swan
Which dances in the snow
White wants to be number one
And doesn't want to go

As white as clouds
As big as the sea
As white as sugar
That drops in your tea

White is the best
White is a wedding dress
That glistens in the sun
Now with luck it's number one

White is ice cream
White is paper
That is as clean as gold
White stands out whether young or old.

Charlotte Tremlett (10)
Days Lane Primary School

Football

Footballs are as big as the sun,
That's why the goals are as long as a blue whale,
This sort of game is mostly for men,
The ball is as bouncy as a spring
And no, they do not go ping.
Keepers diving to their left, to their right,
They are put on the spotlight,
Van Nistelrooy, Crespo and Mutu,
Cudicini, Sullivan and Ambrosio too.
The crowd are as loud as a plane,
Most of them are going insane.

Roberto Faratro (10)
Days Lane Primary School

Slow, Slow Turtles Go

Slow, slow turtles go, they take all day to get to Heathrow,
Slow, slow, they eat your food and they go *oh oh*.
Slow, slow, turtles take years to grow,
Goodness gracious, they are so slow!

With shells as hard as rock,
They smell like a dirty sock.
They come in many colours
And they spend their life at sea,
They really are slow as can be.

Slow, slow turtles,
They live outside their shell,
They sail along so happily,
Like a bobbing buoy,
Slow turtles are a joy!

Jack Gregory (11)
Days Lane Primary School

Bananas

Bananas are yellow,
As squidgy as marshmallow,
It shoots out like a rocket,
It even fits in my coat pocket.

It's as fresh as an ice lolly,
As yellow as the hair of my dolly,
Shining in the sun,
Tastes of my cream bun.

Smells like a jungle,
Gets me in a bundle,
Curved like a crescent moon,
My banana mix will be ready soon.

Lauren Strong-Perrin (10)
Days Lane Primary School

Snow Is Everything

Snow is like a gift from above,
Like fluffy candyfloss
For us all to love.

Snow is as fun as a ball,
As cold as a winter's day,
It's six inches tall.

Snow is like a lucky charm
Sitting in my jewellery box,
It makes the world seem so calm!

Snow is like a vicious fight,
It's as bright as the sun
And as dark as the night.

Snow is like a subtle spice,
But now, it's all ice!

Rachel Wilson (11)
Days Lane Primary School

Green

As green as grass,
As bold as brass,
As green as jade,
The colour of a bucket and spade.

As green as the hills,
As big as mills,
As green as eyes,
Green is the colour for a surprise.

As green as a tree,
As fine as it could be,
Green is the colour of the sea,
Green is a pretty colour, do you agree?

Jade Bristow (11)
Days Lane Primary School

Teacher Mind Control

Homework diary, red list too
Get some folders that are new
Marking pens blue or red
Put in some old pencil leads

PE lessons, playtime sessions
Homework questions
Stir it, boil it, it will bubble
We will never get into trouble

Blue ink, black ink
Bright pink paint
Now we can use the word ain't
Walking, walking, never talking
Now we can run and have great fun

No more homework, no more school
Now the kids control all the rules!

Natasha Ryland (11)
Days Lane Primary School

Orange

Orange is a parrot,
the colour of a carrot.
Orange is the sun
that makes people have fun.

Orange is bright,
as right as a light
which makes people fight.
Orange is the colour
of a flying kite.

As bold as brass.
Orange is the colour for play.
Orange soon fades away.

Richard Hill (10) & Aaron Gannon (11)
Days Lane Primary School

My Budgie!

My budgie is so annoying, he's like a hyena
Having a laughing fit, eating a boxing mitt

He can be as funny as a clown feeling down
He is a person in a budgie suit going to a dance

He is as tall as a pencil going to the shop
As popular as a funky rock star going to a bar

As cool as a cucumber in Menorca
He's like a multicoloured rainbow over the sky
Eating toast like a guy

When you touch him
He's so soft as a feather
In the loft.

Amy Campbell (10)
Days Lane Primary School

My Cousin Bradley

My cousin Bradley is really mad,
He is always happy and he is never sad.
My cousin Bradley is very crazy,
He is always moving and he is never lazy.

My cousin Bradley can be such a tease,
He is impolite and he doesn't say please.
My cousin Bradley can be really daft,
He is very silly and he makes himself laugh.

My cousin Bradley is very funny,
He gets excited when it's sunny.
My cousin Bradley is a bit of a fool,
But sometimes he can be very cool!

Chloe Raggett (11)
Days Lane Primary School

Teachers

Teachers are excellent,
Teachers are great,
But there are some
We don't appreciate.

Miss Ramkissoon marks them out,
Miss Frost too without a doubt,
But some are clever, some are not
And some teachers have lost the plot.

As strict as a lion,
As funny as can be,
As cunning as a crow,
That's just like our teacher, Mrs Lee.

Mr MacDonald and Year 5 too,
All their things are brand new,
If you don't hand your homework in,
Expect too be hung like a pin.

Our dinner ladies are . . . OK,
If you want school dinners you have to pay,
We go out on the field and play,
On a sunny day.

Aron Rieger (10) & Nathan Bowman (11)
Days Lane Primary School

Sport, Sport Is The Best

Playing ball is OK
But I really hate croquet
I really like pool
If you don't, you're a fool.

There's an American sport called baseball
But my favourite sport is football
I really like hockey
But who is the best jockey?

Daniel Furlonger (10)
Days Lane Primary School

The Queen

She smashes many bottles of champagne
Around her place is a red lane
Her corgi died in not much pain
Her money does not bring her fame

She does not spend her money on diamond rings
Hats are one of her favourite things
She is as posh as a caviar
She says to the press blah, blah, blah

She is as slow as a snail
She cuts many red ribbon
Sometimes the press are hidden
The cameras don't last as time goes past

She has had many jubilees - bronze, silver and gold
We are now told she's getting old!
She is as well known as can be
Which is why she has high security

We love our Queen, we love our Queen
She is royal in every place she has been.

Bret Stanley (10) & Tom Bassett (11)
Days Lane Primary School

Monster Teacher

We have a monster teacher,
Who is as round as a pizza,
She is as tall as a rainforest tree,
She likes the odd cup of tea,
With a biscuit on the side,
That's why she is so wide.

We have a monster teacher,
Be careful or she'll eat ya!
She's either man, woman or creature,
If you make her shout,
My advice is *'Get out!'*

Kay Clark (11)
Days Lane Primary School

Fast And Furious

Racers in their cars,
Stereo up full blast,
Spoilers high, bumpers low,
Don't get me wrong, these cars aren't slow.

These cars are as rapid as a rocket,
As sharp as a knife,
The gear stick's there so knock it,
Accelerate and drive.

Exhaust as bold as brass,
With jet tinted glass,
Chrome rims gleaming,
Headlights beaming, like bright shining stars.

These cars are as rapid as a rocket,
As sharp as a knife,
The gear stick's there so knock it,
Accelerate and drive.

V8 engines loud,
Like the deafening roar of the crowd,
Dump valves blowing, engines showing,
Like a candle glowing in the pitch-black dark.

These cars are as rapid as a rocket,
As sharp as a knife,
The gear stick's there so knock it,
Accelerate and drive.

The lights are staying red,
Adrenaline in your head,
The lights have now gone green,
Now you're blowing steam.

Rhys Crane (10) & Eren Arif (11)
Days Lane Primary School

I Have A Dog Called Pippin

I have a dog called Pippin,
Her ears always flop,
She is as brown as brown can be,
Her hair is like a mop.

I have a dog called Pippin,
She is really nice to meet,
Once you get to know her
And give her a little treat.

I have a dog called Pippin,
Her coat is like a winter day,
It wiggles and jiggles,
Especially when she plays.

I have a dog called Pippin,
She can always cheer you up,
She comes to you when you're feeling down,
She is such a special pup.

Rhian Whiting (10)
Days Lane Primary School

My Dog, Ted

My dog, Ted
Has a very big head
He sat on a peg
And broke his leg

My dog, Ted
Sleeps in his bed
He barks all day
Until he gets his own way

My dog, Ted
Has a brother called Ed
He may be a bit dim
But I do love him.

Gemma York (10)
Days Lane Primary School

Lizards

Lizards are cool,
Some climb up the wall.
They get on your nerves,
But they're better than birds.

Lizards are cute,
They're always mute.
Their shredded skin,
Is smooth and thin.

Lizards are quick,
They catch with one lick.
They only bite,
When they're up for a fight.

If you want a friend,
They're best to get.
But the thing they're most good at,
Is being a pet.

Jack Cliburn (10)
Days Lane Primary School

My Dog

My dog
Can leap like a frog.
She hurt her paw
And it was very sore.

My dog
Chases my cat, Mog.
When she goes to bed at night,
Nothing gives her a fright.

My dog
Snores like a hog.
My dog does whine
But she is mine.

Nicole Muskett (10)
Days Lane Primary School

What Am I?

Am I a dog,
Or a hog?
Am I a pig?
Am I a cat,
Or a bat?
Am I a cow
Who moos all day?
Am I a lion or a tiger?
I just want to fight a zebra.

Am I a dinosaur or a mouse?
Am I a rat,
Or a gnat?
Am I a bee who buzzes all day,
Or am I a wasp who stings his prey?
Do you know who I am?
Have a guess if you can.

Billy Holloway (11)
Days Lane Primary School

My Imaginary Brother

My imaginary brother is as crazy as can be,
We try to make him stop, but he's so far out to sea,
He doesn't listen to a thing although he's got big ears,
I know this sentence will seem wrong, but he says he always hears.

My imaginary brother sits around all day,
He's also very nasty, but he always gets his way,
Although he's just a kid, he always drinks his ale,
So if we tried to sell him, we wouldn't get a sale.

My imaginary brother is definitely not my friend,
It's because he drives me round the bend,
When he walks to the park he always seems alone,
You know how I know this?
Because I made him on my own!

Lucan Pearce (10)
Days Lane Primary School

Best Remembered

My sister's bunny rabbit,
My dad's naughty habit,
My mum's small hat,
Mr gran's black cat,
My auntie's scar,
My nan's house is far,
My mum's big hand,
My nan's sparkly fan,
My cousin's baby,
My question is, maybe,
My uncle's nest,
My mum's dog's a pest,
My brother's best mate,
My sister's brilliant fate,
My dad's tie,
My dog's babies will die,
My gran's nice,
My mum's ice,
My brother's smelly feet,
My sister's work is neat,
My gran's dusty scarf,
My best friend's laugh,
My dad's old telly,
My mum's new wellies.

Shelly Parish (8)
Days Lane Primary School

My Four-Legged Friends

My pets are like my best friends,
They comfort me when I'm sad.
My pets are like my best friends,
They calm me when I'm mad.
When I am sighing
Or when I'm crying,
My pets are always there for me.

My pets are my best friends,
They would never hurt me.
My pets are my best friends,
They're as loyal as can be.
Whenever I am feeling happy or sad
Or whenever I am feeling angry or mad,
My pets always comfort me.

My pets are my best friends,
They are the coolest lot.
My pets are my best friends,
I would trade them, *not!*
I'll stick with them through thick and thin,
Even though they make a din.

I have got something to say,
That when we have grown up and gone away,
We will never forget those pets who
Were special to me and special to you.

Victoria Hobbs (10)
Days Lane Primary School

Games Consoles

PlayStation, PlayStation, PlayStation 2,
Many of your games are excellent too.
PlayStation, PlayStation, PlayStation 2,
Lots of children are looking for you.
PlayStation, PlayStation, PlayStation 2,
No other games console is better than you.

PlayStation, PlayStation, PlayStation 1,
No one else can have so much fun.
PlayStation, PlayStation, PlayStation 1,
All of your games bring us excellent fun.
PlayStation, PlayStation, PlayStation 1
You and your games bring us hours of fun.

Game Boy, Game Boy, Game Boy Advance,
The games we enjoy take us into a trance.
Game Boy, Game Boy, Game Boy Advance,
When I look at the screen I can't help but glance.
Game Boy, Game Boy, Game Boy Advance,
I will go to the shops and try my chance.

Nicholas Maslin (11)
Days Lane Primary School

Arsenal

Arsenal, Arsenal, they'll give you a test
Arsenal, Arsenal, they're simply the best
Top of the league and we're staying put
And Henry scoring with his great left foot

We're always thrashing teams 5-zero
Bergkamp, Viera, Parlour, our heroes
Chelsea and Man U are no match for us
At Highbury we'll beat them without making a fuss

Arsenal, Arsenal, they'll give you a test
Arsenal, Arsenal, they're simply the best.

Jamie Francis (10)
Days Lane Primary School

My Brother

My brother is such a pest
He doesn't get off my chest
He really, really hates me
And thinks he is the best.

He always disagrees
And never says please
But when he gets angry
He kicks me in my knees.

My brother watches telly
And his feet are really smelly
But when I get angry
I thump him in his belly.

My brother is so dim
And is the opposite of thin
But deep down inside
I might just like him.

Danny Plummer (10)
Days Lane Primary School

Premiership

The Blues, the Blues, are not far behind,
The Blues, the Blues, Scott Parker has signed.
Trying to stay above Charlton,
Are they worthy of beating Bolton?
The Blues, the Blues, winning all their games,
We're the greatest ones, we are going up in flames.

The Blues, the Blues, have got lovely skills,
The Blues, the Blues, are going for the kill,
We are going to beat Arsenal no matter what,
The Blues, the Blues, are going to thrash the lot.

Samuel Bowden (10)
Days Lane Primary School

The Graveyard

I enter the graveyard.
My heart is racing like a cheetah.
The chill down my spine is as sharp as an icicle,
As cold as a freezer.
The iron gates rattle, like a snake ready to attack.

I hear lots of noises.
Windows smashing, wolves howling, owls hooting.
When I look at the ground, it seems as if hands are sticking out.
I trip over them.
I can't stop panicking.
Suddenly, a bony hand touches me.
I run home as fast as I can.

I can't stop crying.
My mind is playing tricks on me.
I hear shouting.
Maybe it's a warning.
My house is in sight.
I run in it.
It's all over.
All in the past.

Ellie Cruickshank (9)
Days Lane Primary School

My Little Brother

My little brother Liam is very crazy
And he is very lazy.
He thinks he's the best
And never gives me a rest.
He loves playing football,
But he drives me up the wall.
When my brother watches TV
And when I change the channel,
He kicks me on the knee.

Lauren Westpfel (11)
Days Lane Primary School

The Old Dilapidated House

As I entered the dark, dilapidated house
It was as quiet as a mouse.
There wasn't a squeak or a sound
And there was nobody to be found.

I felt as if a ghost or something was watching me
I felt a mouse crawling up my knee.
The rats were nibbling on my shoelaces as I looked up
Could I see spooky faces?

Windows are smashed
And the place is trashed
The floorboards creaked
Water pipes leaked.

I looked up and saw
Brown, rotted skeletons and skulls
Leaning up near the stairs.

Matthew Brown (10)
Days Lane Primary School

My Cat Arthur

Arthur was a friendly feline,
He was always our best cat,
He always followed us
And he was nowhere near fat.

But he developed cancer,
Even though I wanted to try
To get rid of his pain,
But the poor old boy had to die.

One year since the day,
I still think he was as brave as a fox,
I really want to stroke him again,
Even though he's in a wooden box.

Thomas Baynes (10)
Days Lane Primary School

Loving Someone

As we glare into each other's eyes,
Yours sparkle like diamonds,
I am silent,
My heart stands still.

I feel like I'm in a singing contest
Forgetting my lines,
I have a funny feeling inside,
Which won't go.

My face is as red as a cherry,
As I back away speechless,
I run down the corridor,
Breathing nervously, heavily.

So that's what love is!
Butterflies fluttering inside,
I can't stop thinking about it,
I wonder if we'll meet again?

Shannon Counsell (9)
Days Lane Primary School

My Horse Poem

Their coat is as rough as the bark of a tree,
As white as the clouds,
It rolls like a rolling stone,
When you stroke their round, fat tummy,
They feel all bristly,
They gallop like cheetahs.

When they wear their bit and bridle,
They shake their heads madly,
I sit on their back and feel important.
I bounce up and down like a balloon in the sky.
They are big, beautiful animals.

Ellie Sparham (9)
Days Lane Primary School

My Best Friend

My best friend's cat
Had a huge hat.
My best friend's phone,
Had a little bone.
My best friend's bear,
Had some hair.
My best friend's fish,
Was in a big dish.
My best friend's limo,
Came with a hippo.
My best friend's log,
Had a pet dog.
My best friend's hair,
Was covered in pears.
My best friend's cat
Loves sitting on my lap.

Rachel Ellen Featherstone (8)
Days Lane Primary School

Apostrophe Poem

Best remembered:
My cat's cute face,
My brother's PS2,
My dad's gluey paste,
My mum's giant cuddles,
My brother's best programmes,
My cousin's short hair,
My friend's hamster.

Best forgotten:
My best friend's fight,
My brother's fright,
My friend's grazed knee,
My neighbour's enormous tree.

Katherine Pell (8)
Days Lane Primary School

The Haunted Mansion

There is something strange about number 22,
The roof looks half eaten,
The banisters feel alive
And the floorboards creak like an old woman's scream.

The door looks creepy
And is only hanging on by a nail,
The knocker is a lion and looks like he has snarling teeth!

The rooms are dark with cobwebs
And creepy crawlies,
The floorboards creak as the wind whistles on.

The hallway is horrible,
It looks like a dump,
That has fallen on it,
But maybe it's like owner's junk.

As the windows open and shut themselves
The house stands still,
The house is falling apart.

It is like the house is dead
I can't help it,
It just looks like that.

Nese Louisa Redjep (10)
Days Lane Primary School

My Little Sister

My little sister, Maisie
Is very crazy
She is three and a half
And she loves having a bath.

She loves playing games
And she has got a friend called James
But she is very loud
And falls asleep in a crowd.

Sally Born (10)
Days Lane Primary School

Apostrophe Poem

Best remembered:
My cat's happy miaowing,
My dog's playful running,
My mum's kind cuddling,
My dad's funny acting,
My cousin's happy smile,
My grandad's silly jokes,
My sister's dopey poems.

Best forgotten:
My cat's enormous claws,
My dog's bad behaviour,
My mum's grand temper,
My dad's aftershave,
My cousin's stupid films,
My grandad's false teeth,
My sister's grumpy face.

Victoria Camfield (9)
Days Lane Primary School

My Older Sister

My sister's in Year 8,
She's definitely not my mate!
Because she's older than me,
She gets her own house key.

Now she is thirteen,
She is very keen,
To make me get the blame
And then hide in shame.

She never says please
And she always likes to tease,
She's always watching TV
But still horrible to me!

Hannah Camfield (11)
Days Lane Primary School

The Haunted House On The Hilltop

As I wake I get my first arrival
I open and shut the windows to make him feel terrified,
My floorboards creak like an old man groaning
I vibrate the stairs to make him lose his footing.

The boy walks past and skeletons blink as the house lights
                                                        turn on and off
His legs look like they are going to run away from him
Outside the grass is as cold as ice
And the wind whistles as it plays a tune.

My crackling windows look like a pair of blue, bulging eyes
The shining armour of the knight glistens in the sky
My black gate is as still as a cobra who is about to attack.

The roaring, crackling fire stares in his eyes,
Invading rats nibble the left over cheese
The rain bangs on me like someone crying,
I am now shattered like a torn-up piece of paper
As the boy runs back home and my eyes pour down with tears.

Ben Quieros (9)
Days Lane Primary School

Charlton Football Team

Charlton, Charlton when we went down
We had a frown
Since we came up, we won the cup
Since Division One we've worked our way up.

Dicanio will never miss from the penalty spot
Nor will Euell, JJ, Lisby, Cole and the lot
Deano's in charge of preventing goals
Scoring them for us is Carlton Cole.

Terry Scott (10)
Days Lane Primary School

Michael Owen

Michael Owen,
Michael Owen,
His confidence was small at first,
But now it's growing.

Michael Owen,
Michael Owen,
He's always there to score,
When his skill is showing.

Michael Owen,
Michael Owen,
He's swift in the attack,
He's no good at defending,
So he never goes back.

Michael Owen,
Michael Owen,
He's been warned he'll get the sack,
If he doesn't pull his socks up
And play better in attack.

It's the FA Cup Final
And Owen's on goal,
Takes it round Lehmann,
And *what a goal!*

Matthew Dowdall (11)
Days Lane Primary School

Shooting Star

I fly through the darkness of space
And while I soar high up in the sky I speed away
I am as fast as lightning.

When I go on my journey, I see wonderful planets
And I stand out from the others
Because I am as fierce as a lion
And as big as an elephant.

Elliott Roberts (9)
Days Lane Primary School

Apostrophe Poem

Best remembered:
My cat's long face
My best friend's place
My mum's sweet smile
My bathroom's pretty tiles
My chocolate's sweet, soft middle
My sister's strange giggle
My mum's arms around me
My mum's big apple tree.

Best forgotten:
My dad's job not working out
My mum's loud shout
My sister's angry face
My things not in the right place
My brother's face when he's trying to be cool
My mum's stupid, horrid rule.

Louise Kenney (9)
Days Lane Primary School

The Little Black Bunny

The little black bunny sits washing his face
He skips and hops all over the place
He nibbles Mum's roses one by one
Then he goes out and lays in the sun.

The little black bunny plays games each day
When all his friends come out to play
They hop and jump, skip and run
And dance about having fun.

The little black bunny sits on a hill
He twitches his nose, then sits very still
As quick as a flash he turns and takes flight
And suddenly disappears from sight.

Sarah May Langford (9)
Days Lane Primary School

Fire

I burn everything as fast as the speed of light.
With my fire claws,
I knock everything down.
People run and shout,
I destroy everything in my path, because no one can beat me!

My burning brightness blasts, covering the Earth like a nuclear bomb.
As people run away,
I stop them in their path
With my fire tail.
Trees run and scream,
Because of my fright.

I will keep on burning until I fall and never return.
Because the only thing I am scared of,
Is the great, big, rumbling sea,
With its great big and little waves.

Harry Ervin (10)
Days Lane Primary School

The Jaguar

My muscular structure and steel-like frame
Helps me to keep fit and never get lame.
My burning gold coat enhances my spots
The rosettes on my body are flecked with gold dots.

I bring deer to their knees, shaking like leaves,
At the sound of my spine-chilling growl.
I'm a bird in flight as I leap off the ground
Chasing after the herds on the plains.

When people see me they quake in fear
Because sometimes I like a change from deer
You see, you humans, your weapons I fear
For I, the mighty hunter, might become the hunted.

Lucy Fawsitt (9)
Days Lane Primary School

Dog

My body colour is chestnut brown and black.
I swirl round my friendly people as they play with me.
They put my diamond coat on as they take me for a walk.
People pass me and they say, 'Hello.'
When I get home they brush my fur.

My friendly people give me my favourite cuddly toy to play with.
I chew and chew my favourite cuddly toy.
My friendly people give me more to play with.

Amy Elizabeth Moore (10)
Days Lane Primary School

Not A Normal Cat

My cat Casper can't climb trees
But he likes to chase the bees
He destroys the flowers
And he chews my shoes.
If he raced my other cat, he'd definitely lose
He has a right temper, if he can't have his food
He pushes Lola out the way
And she gives him a look to say, 'How rude!'
He snores all night
And trips me up when I turn out the light.
He chases the football across the TV screen
And when it comes to running, he's not keen
Everybody calls him Bagpuss
But I just think that he's a wuss
We call him Fatboy
And he's even too lazy to play with his toys
But he's so furry, he has a brain of a dog
And the amount he eats he'll need a trough like a hog.
He's not like any other cat
But I don't care and that is that.

Gemma Short (9)
Grove Park Community Primary School

Snowing Days

Snow is so fun
Not a time for a bun
Oh! It's hard and wet
Windows have no time to set
In we come, cold as can be
Not a minute to lose not even for a wee
Go, go, go, go outside
Dogs get a time to ride
And have a great time
You and me, fine
Snow, snow come again.

Zara Wilkins (9)
Grove Park Community Primary School

The Snake

Snake slithers through the grass
No one knows where he goes
Through the tree you might see
A flick of his tail
Sssss he goes and *ung* go his teeth
As he bites his prey
Beware of the snake . . . OK!

Robyn-Marie Kenyon (7)
Grove Park Community Primary School

Snow

Snow is white
The children play all night
Making snowmen as they go
One fell down
And the others were melting
In the bright sunlight.

Summer-Paige Walsom (10)
Grove Park Community Primary School

Colours

Gold and silver is for shining coins,
Red is for shining poppies,
Blue is for bright skies,
Pink is for shining sunsets,
Yellow is for the bright shining sun,
Green is for the bright, new grass,
Black is for the dark winter nights,
White is for the sparkling snow,
Brown is for the colour of your eyes that I love.

Reece Michael Allen (8)
Grove Park Community Primary School

My Mum

She's a comfortable beanbag
A mathematic god
A bubbly chocolate
A breath of fresh air
She's a red rose
A soft teddy
She's a doctor when I am ill
A new flower just opened.

Beth Forecast (10)
Grove Park Community Primary School

On A Foggy Day

As I walked outside today
I noticed the sky was grey
I looked on the ground and saw that the grass was white.
Out jumped a dog that gave me a fright.
The fog was so thick that it made it dark.
So I could not see the swing in the park.

Danielle Parry (7)
Grove Park Community Primary School

Summer And Winter With My Friends

I love summer
Sitting under trees
Chilling out
Spending time with my friends.

I love winter
The snow
The time off school to play
With my friends.

That time is precious
It's not here everyday
I enjoy it while I can.

Summer and winter are the
Best times of the year
And
My friends are the bestest
Friends anyone could have.

Robyn Cesary (11)
Grove Park Community Primary School

Harry Potter

Harry Potter is a wizard,
Dobby is a house-elf,
Harry Potter is very strong
He can survive any blizzard!
Hagrid is half giant,
Hermione is very clever,
Ron is Harry's best friend,
No one hates Harry Potter
Never!
Harry is in his 6th year
Of Hogwart's Witchcraft and Wizardry
And Malfoy, Crabbe and Goyle
Are quite a misery!

Rachel Foulger (10)
Grove Park Community Primary School

Snow And Ice

In the morning when I wake up
I see the ice all glistening so much.
And when I go out to play with my friends,
I start to slip and slide and fall down and hurt myself.

I made a snowman all clean and white
And then we had a snowball fight.

My snowman was all bright and colourful.
I had snow all over me and I was very cold.
We got really wet because the snow started to melt
And the snow got all soggy and mushy.
We buried each other's feet in the snow.

My mum came out and said, 'What have you done to yourself?
Come inside, you need to have a bath.'

'No, I'm having too much fun!'

Charlotte Skinner (8)
Grove Park Community Primary School

Night

At night when I can't go to sleep
I open my curtains for a peep.
I see the moon shining bright
The stars twinkling white
And the neighbour's cat's eyes are a scary sight.
Cars blinding me as they go by
People rushing past, I wonder why?
The clouds are darker in the sky.
Trees swaying from side to side
I hear noises I'm going to hide
But it's only the thunder and rain outside.
Why is it dark?
Where has everyone gone?
All cosy in bed until dawn.

Tiffany Sequeira (7)
Grove Park Community Primary School

Lost

Happy birthday to me,
It's my birthday, *whoopee!*
I open a present and what do I see?
A shiny gold necklace just for me,
I put it on,
It's nice and long,
I can't wait for the wedding tomorrow,
It's Auntie Norrow.
The next day came,
I can't find my necklace, oh what a shame.
I'll ask my mother,
Or maybe my brother,
Oh what shall I say,
I'll be punished for the rest of the day.
I put on my outfit,
It's a perfect fit!
I look in the mirror and what do I see?
My shiny gold necklace just for me,
I am a silly twit,
I'm wearing it!

Emma Ripley (11)
Grove Park Community Primary School

Boring School Morning

Usually we have geography or history
Or something boring like that.
Then we have literacy
(Ouch! my fingers are going red)
After that, we have a break
(To get away from the bore).

Then we come in for some hard maths
So that's what our boring school morning
Was like in class 4C in 2003.

Ellena Hurst (9)
Grove Park Community Primary School

White

White is like paper
White is like a ghost
White is like roses
Growing coast to coast.

White is like eggs
White is like clouds
White is like an aeroplane
Flying above the ground.

White is like chalk
White is a candle's shine
What's your favourite colour?
White is mine.

Nardiah Beasley (8)
Grove Park Community Primary School

Animals

A nimals go scurrying,
N ot knowing what they'll find,
I n the wild as they go,
M unching leaves and fruits,
A ll the good things they'll find,
L ook now for somewhere to rest,
S leep, sleep, sleep.

Jamie Emmett (10)
Grove Park Community Primary School

The Wind

The wind is cooling on a summer's day
The wind's a gentle breeze in the month of May
I like the wind as it dashes about
Making young children jump and shout.

Nicola Amy Cook (8)
Grove Park Community Primary School

Up Into Space

I will go up into space
I think it will be a race
I will float around
Without making a sound.

I can see the planets
Earth, Jupiter and Mars
The one thing I didn't see
Were wheels on cars.

It was an amazing sight
Especially on the flight
I like the aliens
They are not like me
They are all green and bubbly.

I'm like an astronaut with the suit
If I had a choice of going into space
Or having a lot of money
I'll tell you now
I'd take the money!

Sammy Singleton (11)
Grove Park Community Primary School

Flowers

Flowers are sweet as a sweet.
I like the blue ones, red, green, yellow and white.
They make me have a big smile on my face
When I see the most beautiful one.
There are so many types of flowers in the world.
Some are weeds, others are just so pretty.
Roses are the most popular ones
Because when they bloom they are so lovely.
Flowers are the most wonderful things in the world.

Jessica Holmes (7)
Grove Park Community Primary School

What Shall We Do With The Naughty Schoolboy?

What shall we do with the naughty schoolboy?
What shall we do with the naughty schoolboy?
What shall we do with the naughty schoolboy?
On a Tuesday morning.

Throw him in a pit with black widow spiders,
Throw him in a pit with black widow spiders,
Throw him in a pit with black widow spiders,
Early in the morning.

Oh dear, he's getting bitten,
Oh dear, he's getting bitten,
Oh dear, he's getting bitten,
Because the spiders are hungry.

Back to the school and the teacher's angry,
Back to the school and the teacher's angry,
Back to the school and the teacher's angry,
Because Timothy's been naughty.

He's locked in a wardrobe with a hungry German,
He's locked in a wardrobe with a hungry German,
He's locked in a wardrobe with a hungry German,
Because he dissed his country,

What shall we do with the naughty schoolboy?
What shall we do with the naughty schoolboy?
What shall we do with the naughty schoolboy?
On a Tuesday evening.

Robert Maxted (11)
Grove Park Community Primary School

Winter Is Fun

W hen the crisp of autumn leaves our nation
I nside by the fire we are
N ice and warm with lots of joy
T housands of snowflakes leave the sky
E verywhere covered with a blanket of snow
R ich, white snow is thrown by the wind

I n our houses we snuggle up in bed
S nowflakes fall outside your window

F un snow fights, I'm ready to join in
U tterly beautiful landscapes of white
N ever ever, will I not enjoy winter, or Christmas
                              when Christ was born.

Samantha Daniels (8)
Grove Park Community Primary School

Thinking

I'm thinking and I'm thinking
This maths is really hard,
I think I've got the answer
But the teacher tells me, 'No!'

I'm thinking and I'm thinking but loads of numbers
Are going through my head
And I'm getting more confused.

Shapes, telling the time, addition, subtraction . . .
Sometimes the numbers are just so fuzzy.

But I close my eyes and I think again,
I say the answer and the teacher says . . .
'Yes!'

Lucy Katherine Horne (9)
Grove Park Community Primary School

The Dog

There once lived a dog
And his name was Dean.
Dean slept on a log
And Dean ate lots of beans.

Dean played with his toys
And played all day.
Dean was a good boy
And never ran away.

Dean Rogers (7)
Grove Park Community Primary School

The Sky Is Blue

The sky is blue,
The sun is shining,
The flowers are blooming,
All the seagulls are flying over the sea,
Lots of animals get born,
Lots of things happen.

Vanessa McLane (7)
Grove Park Community Primary School

Winter

Winter is snow, like a flock of sheep,
When flowers just begin to peep.
When I look out of my window,
I see nothing but the colour of dough.

I see children play all day,
While the clouds make their own milky way.
Children take their sleighs up on the hill,
When some look up at the iced-up mill.

Bronwyn Shishkin (9)
Ightham County Primary School

A Snowy Day

Snow has fallen.
Just outside I can see
The Christmas tree
Covered in snow
Still rich green.

Further down the garden
I can see
The dead rose tree
And the rosemary
With a pot edged with snow.

Near the back fence
I can see the tall pine tree
Swaying in the breeze.

Beyond the garden's boundary
I can see
A snow field
As white as crystal.

In the far distance
I can see
The bare trees
Of the bluebell wood.

Carys Herbert (7)
Ightham County Primary School

Horse

Owner on a horse using a rein.
Galloping forever across the plain.
Running through trees and on grass.
Saddle on back and tail like brass.
Running so fast, fur so soft.
Loud, hard noises, no time to cough.
Cars whizz by, engines and wheels.
Horse gets scared and gives a squeal.

Shannon Thomas (9)
Ightham County Primary School

If The World

If the world were black and white,
There would be no day or night,
If flowers were 20 feet tall,
Trees would be so big they would fall
If humans had beautiful wings,
There would be no aeroplanes, even for kings,
If the world had no sea,
Fish would have to climb a tree,
If the world was twice as big,
You could eat a giant fig,
If the world had no night,
It would be awfully light,
If a beetle could eat a cat,
A flea could eat a bat,
But if any of this was true,
Most of us would not exist.

James Hayman (11)
Ightham County Primary School

When The Last . . .

When the last snowdrop falls,
The first crocus blooms.

When the first crocus blooms,
The first honeybee comes.

When the first honeybee comes,
The first nectar is taken.

When the first nectar is taken,
The first honey is made.

When the first honey is made,
The first jar can be filled.

When the first jar is filled,
I can have some for my tea.

Hattie Linley (7)
Ightham County Primary School

Autumn Thoughts

Leaves are turning golden brown
Conkers and chestnuts falling to the ground
The chilly air is very breezy
Grannys and grandads are getting wheezy.

All the squirrels gathering nuts
The freezing breeze blows the doors shut
The leaves are flapping on the branches
The trees are making little arches.

Animals hide in the ground and in the trees
They are sleeping soundly under the leaves
Leaves begin to turn yellow and red
Lots of people are snug in their beds.

Summer has gone
Autumn is here
All the leaves change at this time of year
Foxes run, rabbits fear.

Hannah Hawkins (9)
Ightham County Primary School

My Teacher

My teacher's called Miss Tart
I like her very much
Her favourite subject's art
And she speaks English and Dutch.

But all the other teachers
Like Miss Rift and Mr Cridget
Hate me and all my features
The worst is when I fidget.

Now here is my conclusion
The only one I've got
My teacher is my solution
All the other teachers are not!

Natalie Stroud (10)
Ightham County Primary School

Spring!

Sitting in the fresh spring air,
Seeing the ants scattering by,
With crumbs on their backs,
The brave little snowdrops,
Scurry back into their dirty beds,
Daffodils push their little heads
And look at their surroundings,
Spring is coming up,
Winter's going back.

Winter awaits its next turn,
To pinch at people's noses
And cause fires to be lit
And smoke to arise,
It causes colds and coughs
And winds all around,
To cause little drafts,
That slither up your clothes
And then it stops to settle down
And lets spring have its turn.

Spring comes and warms the day
And causes winds to stop,
Then flowers come to visit
And brighten up our world
And a sweet scent floats around
And makes us friendly and smile,
The daisies smile
And the buttercups grin,
Spring is a lovely, lovely time
And everyone should praise our world!

Georgia Marsh
Ightham County Primary School

My Garden In Snow

Snow has fallen
Just outside I can see
A wall of mud, frozen hard
With snow in its cracks
Which sparkle and shine
Dead plants, black and brown
Bending like an old man's back.

Further down the garden I can see
A tree with no leaves
Standing alone in the sun
Covered in snow
Like a white skeleton.

Near the back fence
On the climbing frame
A collared dove
Cleaning its feathers
The bamboo's green leaves
Swaying in the wind.

Beyond the garden's boundary
I see a field covered in snow
Melting at the edges
Where the trees grow
A fence all the way round
Where no snow would land.

In the far distance
I see no birds in the sky
I hear pigeons calling -
The only thing I can hear
Except for the wind.

Owen Herbert (10)
Ightham County Primary School

Winter And Summer

Winter is when we wrap up warm
And not like summer when we lie on the lawn.

Winter is when the cold hits our faces
And not like summer when we pack our cases.

Summer is when the flowers grow
And not winter when the flowers are low.

Summer is when we all feel hot
And not like winter when the sun's not out a lot.

Winter is when we eat hot food
And not like summer when we're in an ice cream mood.

Winter is when it's always raining
And not like summer when we're always boiling.

Summer is when we go to the zoo
And not like winter when that's what we hate to do.

Summer is when we're always outside
And not like winter when we're always inside.

Winter is when snow can fall
And not like summer when we play beach ball.

Winter is when we play in the snow
And not like summer when we hear the crows crow.

Summer is when we go on holiday
And not like winter when we're waiting for May.

Summer is when we swim in the sun
And not like winter when we're trying to have fun.

Rosanna Cousins (10)
Ightham County Primary School

London

London is a busy place,
With buildings tall
And full of grace,
Busy roads, busy shops,
Posh clothes with lots of lace,
Here's a restaurant full of food,
There goes by a slow bus,
Hardly any people are rude
Off I go on a tour,
Past all places,
Glowing with glory,
London.

Ione Storey (10)
Ightham County Primary School

Fairies And Pixies

F airies are everywhere
A round and about
I n and out
R ising up
I n the flowerbeds,
E veryone wishes they could
S ee and touch them

A nytime, any place,
N ight or day,
D arting about

P rancing and dancing
I n between the trees,
X cited, they run
I nto the forest
E ager to watch the beautiful
S etting sun.

Catherine Bevan (11)
Murston County Junior School

Love Of A Rose

The love of a rose is from your heart.
You have someone special to start.
The rose's red petals make your heart have a gift.
The love makes you feel like you are going to be lift.
Love is a miracle, you can be fallen.
Your one desire's heart will be stolen.
A handsome boy will spot your heartbeat,
He'll lift you off your own two feet.
The rose itself is cherry red.
'Your beauty,' he said.
Love came alive!
I need you to make me survive.
Say the word love.
You will fly like a dove.
Say what you say, that love is a bird.
Feel like a wild horse's herd.
The rose will save you from a broken heart, you feel sad.
But when the rose is yours, then you are mad.
Life a soft cat, you will pounce.
But like a heart, will bounce.
Do the angels get the love?
Or the Devil will get rough.
The love gave me a sign.
For my special Valentine.

Jessica Emptage (10)
Murston County Junior School

I Will Put In The Box . . .
(Based on 'Magic Box' by Kit Wright)

I will put in the box . . .
The colours of the sunset,
The baby's first laugh,
The first snowdrop in the whitest Christmas.

I will put in the box . . .
The last word of a dying dad,
A baby's first cry
And a shivering snowman.

My box is made of . . .
Icicles glittering in the sun,
Sparkling gold and silver,
The hinges are made of glittering oysters,
The joints are made of tiger's bones.

Natasha Wimble (10)
Murston County Junior School

The Best Fairy In The World

I'm a little fairy sitting in a tree,
Watching all the people staring up at me.
My pretty pink dress and light, airy wings,
You think they would be smiling with big, cheesy grins.
But the snow, it is falling,
Upon each little nose
And it's freezing them, right through to their toes.

So here's some of my fairy dust,
I will sprinkle it about
And if it works they will scream and shout,
Screams of joy,
Screams of laughter
And tears of happiness.
All of which I'm sure would show,
I am the very best.

Hayley Eve Elliott (10)
Murston County Junior School

I've Got A Monster

I've got a monster under my bed,
He's always giving me a fright,
He looks a bit like my friend Ryan,
Which really is a sight!

He's horribly green and scaly,
With a squashed tomato nose,
With blue button eyes and purple hair
And is always picking his toes!

He's haunted me since I was three
And caused me no less than hell,
So if you hear groans under your bed,
He might be haunting you as well!

Chloe Smith (10)
Murston County Junior School

The Rain

The rain *plops!* as it falls to the ground
It leaves puddles like dirty and clean ones.
The rain is a pain when you want to go outside to play.
The rain starts to pour and then starts to spit
As a shower goes on and off.
As the beautiful rain falls, the clouds start to move
Like they are fed up with the place.
The clouds are like cotton wool
At night-time you can't see the rain
Because it's so dark
The rain hears the dog bark
It's a big dot in the sky.

Megan Locker (9)
Newington CE Primary School

The Crescent Moon

The crescent moon is like a giant shining star
Twinkling in the sky.

The moon is like a magnificent light
High in the sky.
The moon is like a golden fish
And the sky is the sea.

The moon is like a magical lantern
But it doesn't just light up the place it's in
It lights up the world.

The moon's best friend is the sun
And they both take it in turns
To light up the world.

The moon is as fast as a shooting star
Whizzing through the air.

The moon is as bright as the sparkling sun.

The moon is a wonderful thing
It is very shiny and bright
And it lights up our world.

Emma Jennings (9)
Newington CE Primary School

Dogs

Dogs are like frogs hopping around,
Like hedgehogs creeping silently.
Their bark is loud, loud and free.
Dogs can run faster than me.
While I jog along, dogs run fast as the wind.
I want a dog that does all these things but . . .
I've got a rabbit that I can cuddle.

Daisy-Mae Cole (8)
Newington CE Primary School

One Day I'll See A Snowflake

One day I'll see a snowflake descending in the breeze.
It would be swaying and floating gently downwards.
It would be white.
As white as the whitest cloud.
As white as the creamiest milk.

My snowflake would be colder than the winter weather.
My snowflake would feel smooth and soft.
It would be gleaming with crystal-clear diamonds.
It would shimmer in the glittering sun.
My snowflake would never melt.
My snowflake would be the best ever born.
To have a snowflake would be my dream.
My snowflake would fall gently into the palm of my hand.

My snowflake would be as small as a crumb.
My snowflake would be the coldest of them all.
It would come with me wherever I went.
My snowflake would run with me when I go to the park.
It would never leave my side.
My snowflake would be the best!

Ellie Pinnock (8)
Newington CE Primary School

Moon

A moon is a bouncy ball, bouncing here and back again.
A moon is a big eyeball looking at you.
A moon is a custard pie, waiting for you to eat it.
A moon is a shiny face staring at you.
A moon is a big, white ball stuck in the sky.
A moon is a big apple waiting to fall down.
A moon sometimes changes shape.
A moon sometimes looks freaky.
A moon is sometimes dull and sometimes shiny.
A moon sometimes looks like it's going to fall down.

Michaela Louise Hearnden (8)
Newington CE Primary School

Roses

Roses bloom when the summer starts,
It opens up like a fairy inside.
Roses have sharp thorns, as sharp as a needle,
The thorns are like darts when you throw them at the board.
Roses are as red as blood.
Roses smell as sweet as summer air as it blooms.
Roses glitter in the sunlight as the sun spreads across the petals.
What a sight it would be
If you touched the sweet, soft petal on the rose
It would be a sight
Oh boy, oh boy.
Oh how beautiful the rose would be
If it would be like someone dancing.

Natasha Clia Elliott (7)
Newington CE Primary School

Pick A Rose

A rose has got lines and is cupful round
The breeze of its whistle is its sound
It's like a baby crying
Or someone asleep, only lying
It's like a ball rolling across the floor
But it's nothing like the size of the door
It can fly away
But its scents will never go away
Not one minute they will stay
Growing up to be as tall as a flower
They'll stay alive another hour
They'll never die and lose their power.

Annabel Rose West (7)
Newington CE Primary School

The Thunder Cat

The thunder cat
Is not fat.
Sometimes you feel as if you hear his growl
It feels sometimes like he's scowls.
It is as if he is having a cry,
You feel like you'll sooner die,
It feels like he's in his wonder,
Which makes me ponder.
Is there a thunder cat,
Or are people saying that.

Bronwen Mary Barton (8)
Newington CE Primary School

My Brother

My brother is a pain,
As horrible as a drain.
As crazy as a bunny,
But also very funny.

He is very silly,
As silly as a Billy.
He makes me laugh,
As we walk along the path.

My brother frightens me,
Like a *buzzing* bee.
He is very nasty but nice
And likes eating rice.

My brother is *great!*
Even though he's not my mate.
He's nearly five
And he's learning to dive!

Megan Rich (9)
North Borough Junior School

A Boomerang

Throw
　That
　　Boomerang!
　　　Watch it
　　　　Fly through
　　　　　The bright
　　　　　Sunny
　　　　　　Sky!
　　　　　　　Stun
　　　　　　The
　　　　　Animal
　　　And
　　Kill it
　　With
　Your
　Sharp
Spear.

Ben Smith (10)
North Borough Junior School

My Hamster

I love his little nose and ears.
His little nose so damp and wet.
He is so, so sweet.
He doesn't keep his cage neat!
He makes a lot of noise at night.
But he would never bite.

Me and my brother taught him a trick.
But he can't run after a stick.
He licks his lips once he's eaten.
He squeaks sometimes like a beacon.
He's sometimes cold because of the weather.
But I love him all together.

Hannah Crickmore (9)
North Borough Junior School

Something Not Serious

Boys and girls
I come behind you
To stand in front of you
And tell you something
I know about.

Next Friday
The day before Wednesday
There'll be a boys' meeting
For girls only.

Wear your most rubbishy clothes
If you have some
If you stay at home
Please come.

Admission is not free
You just walk through the door
We will give you a bench
You must sit on the floor.

It makes a difference
Where you sit
The kid in the second row
Is sure to kick.

Ronnie Angel (9)
North Borough Junior School

Gentlemen

G reat are the men
E ach one has a den
N ow and again they come out
T o spread their arms and start to shout
L adies singing in their ears
E ach one singing about their fears
M aking them start to freak out
A nd chasing them all about
N ever again, the men started to doubt.

Tom East (9)
North Borough Junior School

Boomerang

                    I
                  Threw
                 My
               Boomerang
             It came
            Right
           Back to me
          It was as
         Quick as
        A buzzing bee
       And hit me
          On the knee
           I tried
             Not to
              Shout
                Get out
                 Of the way!
                  But I could
                    Not stop myself.

Claire Beevis (9)
North Borough Junior School

Under The Ocean

Under the ocean
You can see the great blue water
You can swim with dolphins
And you can swim with whales.
If you swim out
In the dark side of the ocean
You see different coloured fish
You also see pearls in their shells.
You see loads of sea creatures
And other special features.

Kirstie Humphrey (10)
North Borough Junior School

My Fish

My fish lives in a bowl
But not in a hole
It has coloured gravel
That will always travel
When it swims around and around
I feed it every day
But in a certain way
I have to change the water
Otherwise it does a summersault with her daughter
My fish is important to me
Because it is golden and sweet.

Gemma Saunders (9)
North Borough Junior School

A Mouse

Mousey, mousey in your housey
Eating cheese and crackers,
Along comes a cat who
Sits on your lap
And eating your lovely green hat.
There is only one crumble
And you get a big mumble,
Sitting there eating your lovely
White cracker.

Kara Emily Fox (9)
North Borough Junior School

David Best

This is the story of David Best,
Who never, ever changed his vest.
He was never clean, but always dirty,
But one day when he was thirty,
He decided he had had enough
Because his girlfriend called him Scruff!
So he went to the corner shop
And was chased back out by a lady with a mop!
David Best ran away and fell in a river,
He was dragged out and ended his days eating liver.

Katie Young (10)
North Borough Junior School

The World's Waking Up!

I hear birds singing in the trees
I hear the buzzing of the bees
Buds are turning into flowers
Creatures are playing for hours and hours.
Spring is here!
But sadly it will go
And turn into summer
When the sun will glow
Too hot for me!

Emma Bunch (10)
North Borough Junior School

Harry's Holiday

When Harry and I went to Spain
We saw a boy whose name was Wayne
We thought he lived in Spain
But it turned out he was too much of a pain
When he wrote us a letter
We thought he could do better

Dear Harry
I have not seen you for a while
And I have a new friend whose name is Nile
Here it is very hot
And I think I am growing a spot
I have to go now
See you soon.
    From Wayne.

Liam Misson (9)
North Borough Junior School

Open Your Eyes And Feel With Your Hands

Open your eyes to see the world
Trees, flowers and animals
Pick the flowers and see all the colours.
Open your eyes
See children playing
Feel their hands
You can touch and see lots of things
You can read books, paint and draw
With your hands.
You can see birds, trees and flowers
With your eyes.

Saffron Ord (9)
North Borough Junior School

Horses Stables

H ailstones and rain are falling on the stables
O ff come the tags and all the labels
R ain and hailstones soon stop falling
S hoes are put on the horses and people start crawling
E veryone is taking courses
S hoes are clip-clopping on the ground while people are riding
                                                  the horses.

S till the shoes are clip-clopping
T hen some rabbits come hopping
A nd the horses go to the stables
B ut there are lots of broken chairs and tables
L ots of food is eaten, but mostly the hay
E aten by all the horses. They don't have to pay
S oon they are given more and then some start to neigh.

Anna Stevens (9)
North Borough Junior School

Jungle

I'm running through the jungle
What can I find?
Over there a lake
I think that I'll have a swim
Run; make way
There's a stampede
Where will I hide?
Look a tree; I'll be safe up there
I can see a lot up here
There's a bird, teaching her young ones to fly
And there's . . . Mum, Dad, I'm up here!

Francesca Evans (9)
North Borough Junior School

The Boomerang

The
    Boomerang
        Skimmed
            Through
                The air
         And
        Sliced
    The
Leaves
Off the
    Trees.
        All
            Of the
                Animals
            Hid because
        They heard
    The boomerang
Coming.
Bump!
    It
        Hit a
            Kangaroo
                Poor old
                    Kangaroo
                        It's stunned now!

Tim Thorne (9)
North Borough Junior School

Sophie's Beard

Sophie ate so many flies
She's chomped fifty-four legs
And two-hundred eyes
She saw one on her bedroom wall
And ate it in a blue dough ball.
A few days later
She looked awfully weird
She had grown
A fly's beard.
She went downstairs without knowing
Her mum was sat down
Knitting and sewing.

George Coster (10)
North Borough Junior School

A Didgeridoo

Once I had a didgeridoo
But when I got it
I was too small to play it.
So I waited for many years
To grow a bit every birthday
One day I will grow
So I can play
On my *didgeridoo!*

Jack Kiernan (10)
North Borough Junior School

Christmas

Every night on Christmas Eve,
Santa comes to stay,
He drops a present then he leaves
And drives off in his sleigh.
He disappears behind the moon,
Thinking of children's faces,
He promises to be back soon,
Then he flies to different places.
He then drops off more lovely things,
To children big and small,
He waves goodbye and happily sings,
'A merry Christmas to all!'

Isobel Emery (9)
North Borough Junior School

Like

A spiky cat like a hedgehog.
A smooth rabbit like some velvet.
A rough, fluffy dog like a big, furry coat.
A white ghost like a sheet.
A bit of slime like a swamp.
A robot like a human.
Hair like a bit of froth.
Eyes like the blue sky.
A new pair of shoes, shiny like silver.
A light as bright as the sun.

Joe Hollamby (9)
North Borough Junior School

What's On The Menu?

They are having carrots today.
And mouldy Brussels sprouts.
I'm having potatoes,
Big, fat potatoes
Because they are juicy, juicy
And potatoes are good for you.
Once I start eating potatoes
I can't stop eating potatoes
Because they are very, very tasty.
Munch, munch, munch go the potatoes
In my mouth!

Ryan Jeffreys (10)
North Borough Junior School

My Best Friend

My best friend has locks in her hair
My best friend is called Emma
My best friend is like a cuddly bear
My best friend makes me happy in bad weather
My best friend is really kind
My best friend is great at singing
My best friend is the best you can find
My best friend is always ringing
My best friend has a nice smile
My best friend has hazel eyes
My best friend is good at a trial
My best friend always tries.

Abby Winter (10)
North Borough Junior School

My School

N orth Borough school is the best
O bviously better than the rest
R ather smart for all to see
T eachers around the school feeling really pleased
H ead teacher called Miss Trickett

B lackboards full up with words
O r sums, experiments too
R eal fun for everyone
O rganised work in folders and books
U nderline the date please
G eography in India
H appy faces everywhere.

Jayde Crittenden (9)
North Borough Junior School

The Boomerang

The boomerang
Flies like Superman
It's sort of bent
But it has a hard end.
It hit a bear
(I am full of fear)
Now's the time to hit the bear
With my spear
That is the end for the bear.

Abinash Joshi (9)
North Borough Junior School

Puppet

She wonders why her head is so high,
She thought it was, she couldn't tell a lie.
She jumps around from place to place,
Trying to remember her own face.
She wishes she could be a bird
And fly around without a sound to be heard.
She wishes she could be a single blade of grass,
Swaying and watching the world go past.
She sits alone in the dark,
Leaning against the gate in the park.
Whenever she feels a pull,
Her strings curl her into a ball.
She looked round a hill
And felt a sudden chill.
After that, she wasn't the same,
When she got home, she saw her photo in a frame
And all of a sudden, she was *gone!*

Zoe Butchers (10)
North Borough Junior School

The Greedy Girl

There once was a girl,
Who ate in a well,
She ate too many cakes
And she turned into a cake herself,
Then, when she got home she ate the telephone,
Just then a human came in and saw her
And he attacked her and devoured her
Piece by piece.

Sam Jeffs (9)
North Borough Junior School

Roar, Roar Tiger

Roar, roar tiger
Where do you go?
Jungle sir, jungle sir,
Don't you know?
Searching, creeping
Upon its prey
Pacing, waiting
For the day.

Liam Chapman (10)
North Borough Junior School

The Blitz

Deafening sirens sounding
A million hearts pounding
The patter of feet from every corner of London
Charging to safety.

Aeroplanes dodging overhead to save their country
While the smoke swirls around
Screaming children to their mothers side they bound.

Shouting wardens appear
The full street seems to disappear
Some down to the underground.

The bombing starts
The bombs shoot towards the ground like darts
Nobody dares look out.

The bombing suddenly stops
People start to come out
When the warden shouts
The blitz has begun.

Ursula Evans (9)
Plaxtol CP School

The Dark And Gloomy Wood

There once was a path in a dark and gloomy wood,
That only the spirits would use.
The trees have taken over, the path is no more,
But you may still hear, the clip-clop of hooves,
As long as you don't disturb the quietness of this place.

The badgers hide away in their woodland realm,
Where nothing can find them, neither spirit or man.
The moonlight shines upon this dark and gloomy wood,
But no one will enter the place,
Because it is known where the spirits play.

They chase each other up the trees and swoop back down,
Some wonder around as if they are lost, crying out loud.
The spirits are stuck in the wood but long for life,
The path is no more, they cannot find their way out,
Forever to haunt this dark and gloomy wood.

Christopher Bowles (10)
Plaxtol CP School

Lost Woods

In the deep woods there was a light which came from the sun,
There was a badger shaped like a bun,
If you went there you would hear the bees,
You would see them round the trees,
As the morning comes to an end, the night-time falls,
The trees grow darker and the grass grows tall,
The purple violets are lying on the ground
Holes lying all around,
Eyes peering out of the holes, trees and grass
The wind runs past,
The birds fly by you, hear the whistles from them,
If you go to the middle of the woods,
You can see the glistening, glittering moon,
Shining on all the trees.

Alia Kassem (9)
Plaxtol CP School

Losing Hope

If you walk into the woods
You will quickly come back out,
The beauty will surprise you
But you'll retreat without a doubt.

There is a stream that flows,
It trickles down the slope,
But as you stand there staring
You will start to lose your hope.

The animals will not see you
For they live in their past,
But your love will soon draw out of you,
It's sure to happen fast.

The birds will just be still
For there's a secret that they know,
But when you see their beauty
Your happiness will go.

When you come out of the woods
You will have your soul no more,
You'll be amongst immortals
Or were you not human before?

Mattie Cracknell (10)
Plaxtol CP School

Memories Of The Woods

In the woods there are noises.
The noise of a horse.
But most animals don't fear.
Going around finishing its course.
Spirits whooshing around in the dark.
Rabbits' ears twitching in the shadows.
Twigs rubbing together, rough against bark.
The river seems deep, but is shallow.

Reece Plummer (9)
Plaxtol CP School

The Members Of The Wood

The guards protect the woodland
Watching everything with care
For they are watching you all the time
Even if you are not there.

The badgers are lively and playful
But they are also gentle and calm
Yet they are very defensive
In the black and white tail suits they charm.

The stream will flow and trickle
It likes to be left alone
It wouldn't like to be disturbed
For the forest is its home.

The woods are famous for spirits
In the distance you hear their call
And there's the faint hooves resounding
On the forest's mysterious floor.

Natasha Holberton (10)
Plaxtol CP School

Blue

The giant blue sea near the beach,
Where small children need to reach,
For the blue beach ball flying through the air,
With happiness and not despair,
On their blue boats the fishermen look,
For nice, big fish to cook,
Massive blue whales chomping along,
Eating plankton, won't take long!
Small seagull's flying overhead
Pestering people to be fed.

Albert Chilman (10)
Plaxtol CP School

The Lonely Man

The man reached for the scratchy handle,
He opened the door of the church,
He wanted to go and pray,
Because he felt inside him he hurt.

As he picked up a book of prayers
And began to sing,
He felt the pain in him grow stronger,
As he sang this beautiful hymn.

But while he was still singing,
He could sense someone was there,
So the man looked round to check,
But glanced into thin air.

The man carried on chanting,
Crooning this graceful song,
But by the time he was halfway through,
The lonely man was gone!

Olivia Betts (11)
Plaxtol CP School

A Flower

A flower stands so tall
It is so beautiful it is like a sunset.

It shines with beauty
And pours with joy and it still stands tall.

Not so small but very tall
When it rains it does not die
It is so strong all the time.

Robyn Clarke (10)
Plaxtol CP School

The Blitz 1941

Deafening sirens wailing,
The sound of a screeching brake,
Wardens shouting a warning,
After the ear-piercing siren, people awake.

The underground shakes so violently,
Their hearts start to pound,
Shock and fear run through their minds,
Tears of joy and sorrow
As they re-approach the ground.

The sight of houses burning,
Their faces pale in fright,
Children cling to their mothers' skirts
At the sight of ruined houses,
Some of them knowing
They would have no homes tonight.

Emily Crawford (11)
Plaxtol CP School

The Blitz

As sirens sound,
Children hurry to their mothers.

Children huddled by their mums,
As bombs drop.

Smoke, dodging inside
The buildings.

Aeroplanes sitting like a bird
About to fly.

Elizabeth Pearce (9)
Plaxtol CP School

The Old Woods

As night-time falls in the darkened woods,
The leaders watch their world,
For if you were to go to this old place,
You may just hear the gentle walk of the living memories,
While the keepers watch their only home,
The animals walk the path,
That was used many years ago,
But not by any mortal you would know.

Jack Lusher (10)
Plaxtol CP School

Blueness

Silently moves the deep, blue ocean,
Boats docked on this watery potion.
No sound could be heard, not even a few words,
They peacefully fly, the blue-tinged birds.
A sudden strong, blue wave,
Hits the rocky mountain cave.
As the sun slowly rises,
They disappear, the blue surprises.

Polly Coumbe (9)
Plaxtol CP School

Rainbow

Beautiful colours shine down from above
Swooping, looping like a dove
As the sunset reappears, orange, yellow and red
And a little girl's mum tucks her up in bed
As the rainbow rises higher, purple, pink and green
Brighter and brighter shine that strong beam.

Alice Pike (9)
Plaxtol CP School

World War II

Deafening sirens, screeching like kids screams.
Aeroplanes crashing through the smoky grey air.
People bustling in and out for safety.

In the distant sky.
Building stood huddled together hoping to avoid.
Posters hanging on one pin surrounded by black dust for attention.
Smoke drifting through the rotten, creaky, burnt wood.

Rubble cramped round the smoky and crushed bricks.
Burnt houses lying hopelessly in the dusty, bashed ground.

People's faces as grey as the sizzling ashes.
Lost ones looking for the loved ones.

Raid after raid happened with every night.
Promising evil lay across the black and gloomy sky.
People looked for safety but no mortal could they find.

Alex Bolam (10)
Plaxtol CP School

Who's In The Woods?

If you enter the woods at night
You'll surely be amazed
The figures moving through the grass
In the shine of the silvery moon
With hands waving in the mist
Reaching out for you
I'd mind your step or you'll be next
Walking through the dark.

Michael Woodgate (11)
Plaxtol CP School

The London Blitz

Houses burnt like skeletons
Smoke trapping houses together
The sky as grey as pencil lead
The street deserted like an abandoned funfair.
Planes flying over like they owned the place.
Poster warning you about blackouts.
People telling you how to put your gas mask on.

Nicolle Aiston (10)
Plaxtol CP School

The Night Draws Near

The night draws near,
Its cold hand scratches my face.
The stars cluster in the sky
Like Christmas decorations on a tree.
The snow on the ground glitters,
Its soft texture shining like pearls
As the night draws near.

The night draws near.
Choirs of foxes sing
And dogs howl like an orchestra.
The streetlights shine like spotlights
Focusing on the varied concert
Which cuts the silence of the night
Like a knife and makes the silent blanket of snow
Seem out of place,
As the night draws near.

Robert Adams (11)
St James' RC Primary School, Petts Wood

As The Moon

As the moon stares down at the night,
She wonders if everything is normal,
The owls are out, the foxes are hunting,
The mice are squeaking, the badgers are snuffling,
But something doesn't seem right.

As the moon paces through the stars of night,
She wonders if everything is normal,
The babies are wailing, the streetlights are flickering,
The trees are whispering, the dustbins are rattling,
But something doesn't seem right.

As the moon is about to leave,
She wonders if everything is normal,
People are rushing to work
And people are getting up,
She was wrong, everything's perfect.

Ellen Costello (11)
St James' RC Primary School, Petts Wood

The Night Sky

The sun has set in the west.
The sun has said goodbye until tomorrow.
We will see the bright yellow, sunny star.
The moon has come up to say hello
It is the moon's turn to watch the world go by.

The clouds shield the beaming, crystal white moon.
Werewolves howl in the midnight sky.
The moon makes shadows, unique as they are.
The sound is terrifying
But that silence is worst of all.

Nicholas Greenwood (10)
St James' RC Primary School, Petts Wood

The Moonlit Sky

The moonlit sky is darker than ever
The birds' feathers are so bright
The animals seem to be so clever
The shining moon producing light.

The sun is rising into the sky
Whilst the morning bakers cook some pie
The paperboy hands out the paper
While the world wakes up.

Luke Brook (11)
St James' RC Primary School, Petts Wood

Misty Dusk At 12.00

The owls hawk indignantly in the bush
While street bulbs shine over the silver, shining drain.
The clock strikes twelve, the animals come out.
The mammals prowl about the brick square,
The tiger comes out, 'Who will fight me?' he asks,
But you wouldn't dare as he'd munch you in his lair,
Twelve turns into one
Dawn is here.

Ronan Napier (10)
St James' RC Primary School, Petts Wood

Darkness In The Night

When the moon arrives in the sky
The wind from the air blows my tie.

When the scary wolf howls at the moon
I wish the darkness would end soon.

When I see a dashing owl in the sky
I always say, I wish I could fly.

John Hatch (10)
St James' RC Primary School, Petts Wood

The Midnight Moon

The midnight moon is a glowing ball of light
Which slips through the night's sky
Shining on the world below it.
The midnight moon drops its piercing glare
On objects that form evil shadows.
The midnight moon laughs madly
When the sun gently sets.

The midnight moon is the brightest
Most magnificent thing in the universe.
The midnight moon cries
Like a hawk screaming for its food.
When the sun rises in the morning
The midnight moon is gone.

Lucy Pereira (11)
St James' RC Primary School, Petts Wood

The Moonlit Sky

The moon is a beautiful thing
It's when the stars start to sing
Over the rooftops that is where
The shining moon does blare.

The moonlight beams
Through the window it gleams
Out on the lovely sea
And beneath the old oak tree.

The moon descends in the sky
It's time to say goodbye
The sun comes out
And waves about.

As it's time to start the day!

Hannah Williams (11)
St James' RC Primary School, Petts Wood

The Star-Struck Darkness

Darkness is a pure black blanket
Lining the night skies.
A group of spangled stars are its cover
Until dawn can rise.
The children of the moon are big and small
Now the dawn is rising
The darkness is gone, its cover vanished,
We'll have to wait to see the black blanket
And spangled stars.

Alice Ballard (10)
St James' RC Primary School, Petts Wood

Hello Moon

Hello moon, goodnight sun
As the sunset starts
The moon begins to glow like the stars on a clear night
The shining sun slowly sinks
Then the gleaming moon starts to rise
From the other half of the world
The bright sun has now gone away
Now the brilliant moon is so bright, it's like the sun
It is now time to say hello sun, goodnight moon.

Rachel Allen (10)
St James' RC Primary School, Petts Wood

The Shadows

The shadows creep by the men that walk.
Men look like giants stomping graciously on the pavement.
Cats look like tigers crouching, hunting for their prey.
Dogs look like lions wondering where their next meal will come from.
Houses look like dinosaurs bearing their teeth
And slashing with their claws.

Charles Turner (10)
St James' RC Primary School, Petts Wood

In My Night

In my night the stars are diamonds
Scattered on black velvet
Guiding me before night turns to day.
Shining pools of gold light up the night
While the fluffy clouds patch up the moon.
Choirs of wolves croon on the midnight hour.
Crickets whistle by the silver moonlit trickling river
Leaves whisper to each other in the breeze
This is my night.

Katrina Longhurst (11)
St James' RC Primary School, Petts Wood

The Glistening Moon

The moon's eyes are as blue as the ocean,
Her face as round as a lollipop,
Her lips sparkle like the stars,
Her nose as strong as a wall,
Stars surround her like guards protecting a castle.

The night sky is as bright as the stars,
Trees sway as the wind flows past,
The moon still stays.

Joelle O'Neill (10)
St James' RC Primary School, Petts Wood

What's That Sound?

I peered outside to a noisy rustling sound,
The street lights were flickering brightly
Like someone turning them on and off.

A little dog was making a loud sound,
By scrapping his paws continuously up and down the door
Waiting for the owner to let him in.

Grace McCarthy (10)
St James' RC Primary School, Petts Wood

Midnight

The moon shines brightly
In the night sky.
Twinkling stars are hanging high.
The soft breeze putting up a fight
Against the warmth
And the creatures of the night.

Hear the dog bark in the shadow of the night
And the gleam of the moon, spraying light.
All over the world children sleep,
While outside darkness slowly creeps.

The streetlamps close their eyes
And the sun leaps into action
As the moon says goodbye,
Until the night returns.

Catherine Dow (11)
St James' RC Primary School, Petts Wood

Darkness Falls

Darkness falls in the land of shadows.
The shadows become the living,
Their bodies become dead.
The shadows start their ghostly walk.

Darkness falls
Choirs of shadows sing their devilish song,
For the long night walk.

Darkness falls
The shadows return to their bodies.
There is no more singing.
The walk has stopped.

Jack Harper (10)
St James' RC Primary School, Petts Wood

The Nightlife Glistening

The sunset awakens, the night's just begun
It produces the nightlife and darkness above.

The moonlight is glistening in the night
The graveyards open, the zombies fright
The twinkling star up in the air
The night awakens everywhere.

The wolves howl and wander like a bunch of angels singing.
The ocean sea absorbs all light and pushes in like a magnet's pull.

The dark sky wind is whistling
The deep, clear river is swaying
The spotlight lamps are shining
Like the big gates above.

Josh Hughes (10)
St James' RC Primary School, Petts Wood

The World Never Sleeps

Stars scuttle across a black blanket in the sky
They sparkle like their mother, the moon
The pattern they make glows with wonder
Because the world never sleeps.

The moon glistens at what is a dark, eerier world
Smiling as it watches us sleep
This miraculous moon lights up the night
Because the world never sleeps.

The streetlights stand tall as they shine
Casting shadows over everything and anything
Producing little pools of light
Because the world never sleeps.

Charlotte Weeks (10)
St James' RC Primary School, Petts Wood

Monsters

Monsters in the garden,
Monsters in the house,
Monsters in the wardrobe,
One's just killed a mouse!

All the monsters laughing,
They come out everywhere,
Some come out at night-time,
Even in the air!

Monsters in the cartoons,
Monsters in my bed,
Monsters in the TV,
One's just bit my head!

Now that they've all gone,
Yippee! Yeah! Wahoo!
The monsters didn't like me,
But one of them liked you.

Jordan Blackwell (9)
St John's CE Primary School, Maidstone

Spring

When the flowers are pink,
When the grass is green,
When the leaves are brighter than any I've seen.

When the lambs skip happily in the grass,
When people come to watch and laugh.

When the baby birds are in the nest,
When the parents have no time to rest.

When the Easter bunny hops around,
When eggs are found on the ground.

When I see these things appear,
I know that spring is finally here.

Hannah Bailey (9)
St John's CE Primary School, Maidstone

My Poem About My Hamster

I have a little hamster
Wizzy is his name
He likes to run around his cage
And play a funny game.

He runs around his wheel at night
And keeps my mum awake
I wish he'd be a bit more quiet
And give my mum a break!

His favourite treats are fruit doughnuts
Sweetcorn and carrots too
But he stores them in his toilet
Something you and I wouldn't do!

He has a little space restaurant
Where he can go and eat
He takes his nibbles up there
But I never give him meat!

He likes to have a run around
Up and down the hall
But to stop him running out the door
We put him in a ball!

Alexander Roy Milne (9)
St John's CE Primary School, Maidstone

The Little Red Head

I've seen a little woodpecker
Quite near to where I live
His little red head bobbing
Pecking in the trees.

Caterpillars and worms
Are his favourite food
And then I see him
Fly back into his nest.

Kasey Bryen (9)
St John's CE Primary School, Maidstone

Monsters

They come in all sizes, colours and shapes,
Some are even as big as apes.

Some are hairy, some have spikes,
But I've never seen one who rides my bikes.

Some only come out at night,
Some are too scared to put up a fight.

Some have tongues as long as a car,
Some are strong enough to break up a bar.

Some will not hurt a fly,
Some grow tall and come very, very high.

Some are as small as a spot
Some are as wide as a cot.

Some really do like sport,
Some live and stay in a fort.

Are you a monster?

Christopher Bennett (9)
St John's CE Primary School, Maidstone

Holiday

When we are on holiday,
We love to have fun all day.
Some of us like swimming
And in the evening some of us like singing.
Turquoise water,
Around the Rock of Gibraltar.
I like swimming in the sea,
With all the fish around me.
But when the sun sets,
I try to forget . . .
We're going home tomorrow.

Nicola Frost (10)
St John's CE Primary School, Maidstone

Football

Football is the best game in the world
It has league games and the Champions League
It has teams which have skill and tactics
You have training and you may get drenched
You have games, which are normally muddy and wet
It includes fun, hurt and excitement
By hurt, I mean breaking a bone and really bad cuts
Yellow cards and red are only given for bad fouls
Lots of games to come and a lot of fixture lists
Lots of suspense about who's in the team
There's also teams that get relegated and promoted
Lots of cups and lots of tournaments
Lots of goals to be scored
All the positions: defenders, midfielders and strikers
Football isn't just in one country
It's in them all!

Andrew Mark Tingey (10)
St John's CE Primary School, Maidstone

Animal Poem

Ants, who are not plants, eat pants.
Chickens eat worms that are in the kitchen.
Dogs and hogs are usually called gods.
My monkey, who is stupid, is very funky.
My fly wears a tie on his high neck.
Bugs do hug on rugs.
Pigs have long legs to lay eggs.
Freaky tigers eat creepy spiders.
My snake uses his tail to take a fork to make a cake.
Bunny eats honey to fill his tummy which I think is so funny.
Small mouses live in tall houses.

Nicholas Li (9)
St John's CE Primary School, Maidstone

Football

Great footballers and great superstars
Come from England and afar.

Every footballer that shoots
With the contact of their boots
Will lead to a great goal.

All the players who have scored
Never get bored
Of this amazing, skilful game.

Television, Sky and commentaries
Cards, free kicks and penalties.

Coaches, rules and the team's kit
With training that will keep them fit.

Football is the name of the game!
Adam O'Connell (10)
St John's CE Primary School, Maidstone

The Wind

swooping and squealing and howling at night,
The wind sings its song from sunset till light,
Blowing and swaying from tree to tree,
Rustling in bushes, chasing birds and bees.
Making balloons float up to the stars in the sky,
Making kites drift up, up extremely high,
Brushing the grass all to one side,
Up to the rooftop, to the top it will glide.
Tapping on windows and scratching at doors,
Causing trouble and mischief and creaking floors,
Turning warm, fuzzy carpet, into awkward and cold,
The wind is nasty, so I am told.
Watch out and beware when you're out in the rain,
It could be the wind, striking again!
Danielle Barrington (10)
St John's CE Primary School, Maidstone

Fairies Around The Year!

Spring fairy, spring fairy, oh happy I would be,
If you would leave your daisy to come and play with me,
So call up all your fairy friends so that we can meet
And go to watch the sunset before we go to sleep.

Summer fairy, summer fairy, how tall does your flower grow?
Does it grow up high in the sky or on the path below?
Here I stand small and blue and I've never seen a garden plot,
But as I know you've probably guessed that I'm the forget-me-not.

Autumn fairy, autumn fairy, sitting in the tree,
Will your black juicy berries do any harm to me?
Elderberry, elderberry up so high
Oh how I would love to be up in the big blue sky.

Winter fairy, winter fairy, how do you cope in the cold?
Do you hide in flowers? Well, that's what I was told.
How you must wish for spring to come and not the cold, old snow,
But when the spring has come, are you sad to see the wintry world go?

Emma-Jane Taylor (9)
St John's CE Primary School, Maidstone

Monkey

M onkeys have long arms to swing
O n top of trees or anything
N it-picking fleas and tiny mites
K eeping clean whilst having play fights
E ating bananas and lots of fruit
Y ou must agree, monkeys are cute!

Sarah Pole (10)
St John's CE Primary School, Maidstone

The Sun

When I wake up in the morning
And the sun is in the sky,
It looks so big and bright
And it looks so hot and high.
I often sit and wonder,
Why the sun is so far away,
I also sit and wonder,
If it will be there the next day.
When it is summer,
The sun is at its best,
It shines all day, but not at night,
For then it goes to rest.
I'm glad we have the sun
And that it's usually there,
Even though we cannot touch it,
It's big enough to share.
For when I'm cold and lonely
And the day seems to never end,
The sun shines through the clouds,
As if it wants to be my friend.
Make the most of the sun because if it goes,
Which it might,
We won't have any warmth or heat
And of course, no sunlight.
So, when the day is ending
And I've had all my fun,
I'm really, really thankful,
That we've got the . . .
Sun!

Deborah Batchelor (10)
St John's CE Primary School, Maidstone

The Four Seasons

Winter wind pounding against the door
Like someone trying to get in.
Rain, slapping hard against the pavement
Like someone trying to stamp as hard as they can outside.
Lightning beams strike,
Thunder bangs loudly;
But then you also see, snow lying
Like a soft white blanket made of wool.
Trees all bare and not a single leaf in sight.
Then there's spring, the time of growth;
Everything slowly springs back to life
As the sun comes back to the sky.
Animals come back, slowly from hibernation.
Flowers blooming and leaves slowly growing back onto the trees;
Rain clouds drifting away, the harsh wind becomes a slight breeze.
The weather becomes hot and it's summer.
Not a single empty bush or tree.
The blazing ball of fire in the sky;
So bright, blinding,
Heat waves flooding in.
Bright and beautiful flowers,
So hot trying to get cool.
Birds and animals everywhere;
Grass and water glistening in the sunlight.
Then there's autumn.
The bright green and yellow leaves
Turn to deep reds, browns and goldens.
The wind gets colder and soars through the trees.
Leaves all over the horizon;
Crunching leaves,
Rustling trees.
Then, back to *winter!*

Chandni Patel (9)
St John's CE Primary School, Maidstone

Summer Days

Summer days
Go catch some rays.
On the beach
Can you reach the sea?
Go eat a fish
On a dish.
See pollution
Go be a solution
By putting it into the bin.
In the sand
Go get a tan.
Have a blast
It'll last.
Can you skip a stone
When it is thrown?
Go for a swim
Until the sky is dim.
Have a rest
Until you feel the best.
Today's another chance
On the beach to dance.

Michael Kitchin (9)
St John's CE Primary School, Maidstone

Football

Football is a sport
Where you have to score for support
Thierry Henry is the best
Better than all the rest
He plays for Arsenal, the team I support
He has lots of money
And is very funny.

Ashley Usoh (9)
St John's CE Primary School, Maidstone

The Jungle Walk

T hrough the jungle the traveller walked
H ere and there he would hear a squawk
E lephants thumped, snakes talked.

J ungle life was so strange
U nder the leaves there was a range
N oises, mud and little bugs
G orillas lumber through the trees
L ook out, he's about to sneeze!
E verything went flying through the air.

W as that a flying tiger over there?
A pes travel around in big bunches
L ow flying parrots might eat his lunches
K oala bears might be on his back, he better turn around
                                              and check . . .

Maria Miles (10)
St John's CE Primary School, Maidstone

Snowflakes

Drifting, floating to the ground,
Twisting, twirling round and round.

Silently falling one by one,
Try and catch one on your tongue.

Covering houses everywhere,
Children playing here and there.

Roll them up into a ball,
Build a snowman really tall.

Watch them shrink and melt away,
Please come back another day.

Emily Bown (10)
St John's CE Primary School, Maidstone

Dreaming

As I lie in bed
I dream about . . .
Children in the sea
People watching me
Candles in a church
A big silver birch
Me eating ice cream
Then I hear my mum scream
Time to rise and shine
To get to school on time.

Chloe Swan (9)
St John's CE Primary School, Maidstone

Family

F amily are the people we love
A unts, uncles and cousins
M ums, dads, brothers and sisters
I nfants to adults, we grow with our loved ones
L ove all around us
Y oung and old, families are what matter.

Rhianna Eves (9)
St John's CE Primary School, Maidstone

The Foolish Baboon

A baboon was walking along the lane,
He tried to fly an aeroplane,
The baboon crashed
And the plane smashed,
Now the baboon's insane!

Finn Collins (8)
St Peter's RC Primary School, Sittingbourne

The Old, Green Beans

A pile of green beans
Wearing old, funny jeans,
Escaped from their tin
With a big, smiley grin,
Which was wiped clean away,
With the pan of the day,
So now it's bye-bye from
The pile of cooked beans,
Laid out on a plate
For a posh dinner date.

Jack Harding (8)
St Peter's RC Primary School, Sittingbourne

Dreaming

D reams are exciting things!
R eally peaceful
E ven when you're feeling sad
A nd when I dream
M y thoughts are happy thoughts!
I 'm glad that they are not bad!
N ight comes and goes
G reat dream I say, when I wake up for another day.

Nicole Boakye (7)
St Peter's RC Primary School, Sittingbourne

Hockey

H ockey is fast and fun
O ut of this world
C ome on and play
K eeper guards the goal
E veryone is after the ball
Y es! We've scored!

Lewis Atkins (7)
St Peter's RC Primary School, Sittingbourne

I Am The Sun

I am the sun
I shine on you.
I live in many places
I shine in the window.
And I shine in the garden.
I am always with you
I will come back tomorrow
After the moon
And I will shine on you again.

Ellie Haddock (7)
St Peter's RC Primary School, Sittingbourne

Boring Babies

B oring but bonny
A nnoying but adorable
B ouncy but bawling
I rritating but interesting
E xtraordinary but exciting
S creaming but squishy . . .

But I still love them!

Poppi-Anna Marie Conway (8)
St Peter's RC Primary School, Sittingbourne

Sisters Are . . .

S isters are
I rritating
S ticky and sneaky
T ricky trashers
E xhausting with energy
R uthless wreckers

But we still love them!

Lauren Etherington (8)
St Peter's RC Primary School, Sittingbourne

February Evening

Now, in February,
It is windy and cold,
For me inside, it is nice and warm.
Inside by the fire,
It is nice and cosy,
The flames, flick up the chimney.
As I sit by the fire,
Warming my toes,
My eyes begin to close . . .
Zzzz.

Zoe Amy Thomas (7)
St Peter's RC Primary School, Sittingbourne

Homework

H omework is no fun!
O h, I don't like these sums!
M um says, 'Homework first!'
E very night, I've got something to do
W e want to play!
O oops! I forgot to do my times tables!
R eading is not so bad
K ind teachers wouldn't give it to us anyway!

Eleanor Page (8)
St Peter's RC Primary School, Sittingbourne

Strawberry Cake

I love strawberry cake,
With lots of cream in the middle,
Oozing out the sides,
Squishy, creamy, strawberry cake,
Oh, how I love the taste.
Yum!

Catherine Meiklejohn (7)
St Peter's RC Primary School, Sittingbourne

Little Kittens

Little kittens,
Fluffy as mittens.
Little kittens,
Play in the snow.
Little kittens,
Are good fun.
Little kittens,
Jump and run.
Little kittens,
Sleep in their basket.
All tired out
By their busy day!

Beth Tumber (7)
St Peter's RC Primary School, Sittingbourne

Oh Homework!

Oh homework, oh homework!
Oh how I hate you!
How I wish you would disappear,
Whenever you come near.
You're last on my list of things to do,
Oh homework, oh homework
Oh how I hate you!

Chloe Escritt (8)
St Peter's RC Primary School, Sittingbourne

Cheeky Monkey

Cheeky monkey
Swinging by its branch
Leaves blowing off the tree
Climbing up quickly
Hunting for food.

Robert Gibson (9)
St Peter's RC Primary School, Sittingbourne

Who Am I?

I'm lying on the sofa, purring all the time,
I've been sitting there from 2 o'clock, to half-past nine!

For I'm the King of Laziness, the ruler of the chair,
I can lie and stretch and yawn and sleep, without a care!

But when the clock strikes 12 and I am good and ready,
It's then I prowl and stalk and pounce and creep, with my mate Eddy.

I am Lord of the Tom Cats,
Leader of the bedroom mats.

I bet you're wondering what I am,
I am that all time favourite, a cat named Sam!

Jane Hammond (10)
St Peter's RC Primary School, Sittingbourne

Fish

Fish swim all day long in the tank
Looking very bored.
All they do is eat the food.
Hiding in and out of their toys they do.
Blowing bubbles when no one knows.
Their bright colours fill the tank
As they race round and round.
When they smile you can never tell
Because their face always looks the same.

Joshua Wells (10)
St Peter's RC Primary School, Sittingbourne

Dogs Haiku

Dogs have cute faces,
Dogs have long and wagging tails,
I love my dog, Max.

Siân Bradley (10)
St Peter's RC Primary School, Sittingbourne

The Magic Finger

Tom had a magic finger
He pointed it to the sky
Then found himself flying
Way up high.

The higher he went the less he saw
As the wind threw him more and more.

At last he reached his final destination
And landed on cloud nine
To be greeted by the sound of people
'Wake up! It's past school time!'

Charlie Sewell (9)
St Peter's RC Primary School, Sittingbourne

Polar Bears

They magically walk on the ice,
Their fur is so very white and nice,
They have the biggest paws in sight
And they can run as fast as light,
They are polar bears all in a line,
My most favourite animal of all time!

Laura Cox (10)
St Peter's RC Primary School, Sittingbourne

Rugby And Football Haikus

Football is so cool
Playing football on the field
And kicking the ball.

Rugby is wicked
Passing, running and kicking
To win, score a try.

Callum Molyneaux (9)
St Peter's RC Primary School, Sittingbourne

Dream Holiday

I'd like to fly straight to Paris,
I'd be an actress, that's what I'd be.

Yeah, I'd rather go to France
And learn a new, famous dance.

Or what about Germany with the beach
And the sand and the great big sea?

How could I forget Kenya with the great big sun?
It would be a great holiday packed with loads of fun.

All these places are driving me mad
Dad might send me to Baghdad.

Instead of going round to Rome,
I can stay in my home sweet home.

Louise Kahira (9)
St Peter's RC Primary School, Sittingbourne

The Weather

Yesterday it snowed,
Today it will be sunny.
Tomorrow brings more rain,
But I don't care because
I'm eating my bread and honey.

Felícia Lane (9)
St Peter's RC Primary School, Sittingbourne

The Icy Road Haiku

One icy morning
A man walked down the cold road
And he slipped and fell.

Sean Maher (10)
St Peter's RC Primary School, Sittingbourne

A Card For Father's Day

Lets make a card for Dad.
With pictures of things he likes:
Mum and all of us, of course
And cars and motorbikes.

Books, CDs and hi-fi,
Models of sailing ships,
Trees and flowers and gardens,
Bacon, egg and chips.

Write our names inside it -
And what shall we write above?
To the sunniest, funniest
Dad in the world
With loads and loads
Of love.

Deanna Ward (10)
St Peter's RC Primary School, Sittingbourne

I Like The Beach . . .

I like to go into the sea
But not with a sore knee.

On the land
There is sand.

With my bucket and spade
I played.

My mum relaxed
While we packed.

We had to go home
We had a little moan.

Until we were home sweet home.

Larrissa Way (9)
St Peter's RC Primary School, Sittingbourne

My Favourite Game

Netball is my favourite sport
And between two teams is fought,
You only need posts, bibs and ball,
Seven players a side, fourteen in all.

You stand in position on the court
And both teams start with nought,
You shoot goals through the post,
The winning team scores the most.

St Peter's playing Barrow Grove,
We're in blue, they're in mauve,
The umpire's whistle is given a blow,
Bounce and chest passes begin to flow.

By half-time a goal we score,
Followed later by more and more,
We had to make sure to defend,
But we won 4-0 in the end.

Emily Robertson (10)
St Peter's RC Primary School, Sittingbourne

I Love Dolphins

Wish, wash,
Dolphins jumping, reaching the sky,
Their blue is so posh,
They jump so high.
They never, ever say bye bye
Dolphins drink so much squash
And they never, ever
Die!

I love dolphins they jump and splash,
The hit the water with a mighty crash,
Their tails go swish when chasing fish,
In the sun they have so much fun,
During the day their bodies are so grey,
But in the light, they flash so bright.

Alice Lawson (9)
St Peter's RC Primary School, Sittingbourne

Dolphins

I love dolphins they swim all day,
They never stop swimming,
They swim high and low,
In the big, blue ocean.

Dolphins are my favourite sea creatures,
With their rich blue colour lighting the sea,
I love their blue, I hope you do too,
When eating their fish, their tails swish.

Marika Paslow (10)
St Peter's RC Primary School, Sittingbourne

My Dog

He is as hairy as a bear,
But I don't care.
At night he stays in my room until late,
He is my best mate.
He is the best I need,
But can't read.
When I come home from school,
He always greets me and acts like a fool.

Kelly Wratten (10)
St Peter's RC Primary School, Sittingbourne

Frogs

Be nice to frogs,
Frogs are the best,
They are better
Than the rest.
They eat nasty
And beastly bugs
And leave your garden
With kind bugs.

Victoria Ward (9)
St Peter's RC Primary School, Sittingbourne

Squirrel's Nest

In the squirrel's nest,
Deep down,
To the ground,
She awakes,
She looks round and round,
For food to eat,
She finds none on her limbs,
Or on her left or right foot,
Busy squirrel,
Goes out to look for food,
Later on, she comes back to the squirrel's nest.

Miles Hutchinson (10)
St Peter's RC Primary School, Sittingbourne

Jumping Off A Cliff

Wind whipping through my hair
It feels exhilarating!
What's that? Shouts and warnings!
But who cares now?
I scrape my knee but I feel nothing
Tumbling down, bashing my head
Spinning, turning, helter-skelter
Silence, a void, infinite darkness.

Emilia Sage (10)
St Peter's RC Primary School, Sittingbourne

Naughty Nelly

There was a girl called Naughty Nelly
She had the most enormous belly.
Said her mum one day,
'Go out and play,
You're watching too much telly!'

George Butcher (9)
St Peter's RC Primary School, Sittingbourne

Sk8er Boy

He glides through the air with the greatest of ease . . .
Till he loses his *deck* and falls on his knees!

Through his *heelflip* and *kickflip* to *impossible* stunts
Hid pads serve him well, when he lands with a grunt.

Up the series of *vert* ramps, sparks seemingly spit
From the grindpole, when metal-to-metal he hits.

The crowd in the park look on in joy
As they take in the moves of the cool *sk8er boy!*

Charlie Heathfield (9)
St Peter's RC Primary School, Sittingbourne

Winter Is Good Fun

In winter people play snow fights
In winter you can touch the freezing cold ice
In winter you can taste the lovely snow
In winter you can hear the snow crunching like crisps
In winter you can see snowflakes floating like feathers
In winter you can smell the fresh, bitter air.

Emily Burston (9)
Seal CE Primary School

A Poem About Winter Scenes

Looking at the snow, soft like a feather.
Hearing snow touching your window.
Dirty people touching slimy icicles, pointy and sharp.
Sticky snow like candy.
A lit candle that smells like lavender.

Amy Primett (8)
Seal CE Primary School

Winter

Winter is snowflakes twirling like fairies
Winter is snow like sparkling crystals
Winter is a sheet of white snow
Winter is icicles shimmering
Winter is making snowmen
Winter is slippery, freezing ice
Winter is drinking tea, warm and nice.

Hannah Lowe (8)
Seal CE Primary School

Winter Magic

Winter is snowflakes dancing like butterflies
Winter in snow magically falling
Winter is hail gently dropping
Winter is snowmen tricking people
Winter is icicles like crystals.
Winter is a magic time of the year

Sophie Obbard (7)
Seal CE Primary School

Senses In Winter

I can . . .
See a large snowman, as soft as a polar bear,
Hear the sound of crunching snow,
Taste the hot turkey,
Feel the icy cold snow,
Smell the hot chocolate at bedtime.

Oliver Maxwell (7)
Seal CE Primary School

Acrostic Of Winter

W histling snowmen
I cy skidding snow
N ice soft, feathery snowflakes
T iny hard hailstones
E veryone has snowball fights
R olling snow to make snowmen.

Kirby Sammonds (8)
Seal CE Primary School

The Feeling Of Winter

I can see a big white blanket of snow on the grass.
I can hear fairy-white soft snow tapping on the window.
I touch a long sharp icicle.
I smell hot tea when it is cold in the house.
I taste the freezing cold snowflakes on my tongue.
Winter is the coldest of the seasons.

James Coppins (8)
Seal CE Primary School

The Winter Fun Poem

Snow crunching under my wellington boots.
I can see a soft snowman, fat and friendly.
Snow, soft like feathers.
Children laugh as they play snowball fights.
Ice, freezing and slippery.
Air, cold and nippy.

Michael McGinniss (7)
Seal CE Primary School

Wintertime

In winter you see snowmen, cold and stiff,
In winter people wear Wellington boots,
In winter snowflakes fall like leaves,
In winter you can touch the shimmering icicles,
In winter you can smell the fresh, freezing air,
In winter people ice-skate, gliding like ghosts.

Dylan Evans (7)
Seal CE Primary School

Winter Poem

W inter is rolling snowballs like a car's wheel
 I ce slippery and dangerous
N ice fluffy snow slowly falling down
T insel and snowflakes coming down like leaves
E very hedgehog hibernates
R abbits dig for food in winter.

Cy Gadd (7)
Seal CE Primary School

A Winter Poem

W inter is snow falling like fairies
 I cicles sharp like knives
N ippy air making the snow go everywhere
T he snowman in a battered hat
E veryone having fun
R udolph delivering presents to everyone.

Iestyn Gadd (7)
Seal CE Primary School

Fantasy Football

The kick-off starts,
The ball is passed,
The man runs,
He is very fast,
He takes it to the 18 yard box,
He takes a shot,
It is blocked,
By a knot,
It is thrown back out,
The crowd starts to roar,
The goalie is in pieces,
Did they score?
The match is over,
The winning team cheer,
The mums go home,
The dads go for a beer.

Jack Treeby (11)
South Borough Primary School

Football!

Football, football,
Great goals,
Muddy boots,
Kicking balls,
Clean shorts,
Football, football,
Teams playing,
Fans chanting,
Score! Score!
Commentators babbling.

Daniel Baines (10)
South Borough Primary School

Tooth Fairies

Delicate embroidered wings,
With dinky satin shoes,
Some wear cute flower rings,
They come when you're having a snooze.

When you lose a tooth,
They flutter down from the sky,
But only if you are full of youth,
The tooth goes to a mountain high.

Leave the tooth under your pillowcase
And when you awake,
It has disappeared without a trace,
You should never think fairies are fake.

Or they won't come to your door
And leave a little treasure,
If you don't believe their hearts will feel sore
And you will drain their life of pleasure.

Kirsty Ross (10)
South Borough Primary School

Dolphins

Sky-blue dolphins dancing in the deep, cold ocean,
Splashing their tails as they move,
Dancing to the sound of mermaid's voices,
Dancing gracefully together, up and down.

Coming out of the waves to say hello,
Going deep down, down below,
Bobbing in the waves together forever.

Nicola Johnston (10)
South Borough Primary School

Fairies

Weave a magic circle new
Making all your dreams come true
Listen closely you will hear
Fairies whispering in your ear
However far you will roam
Fairy friends will bring you home
Hear the sound of fairy song
Fill my senses all day long
Make each day shine so bright!

Fairy folk will always find
Those whose hearts are true and kind
And so your wishes can come true
If kindness rules all that you do
Let magic words you write by hand
Carry us to fairyland
Fairy magic, fairy song
Perfect sound both sweet and long
Fairy magic all around
Where rainbows touch the ground
Fairy laughter like a bell
Laughter casts a magic spell

Fairies love to dance and play
Catch them and they'll fly away
Wings that shimmer in the light
Soft gowns of pearly hue
Fairy folk that glitter bright
Like drops of morning dew.

Tasha Atkinson (10)
South Borough Primary School

Famous People Poem

Once there was a footballer
Who was popular
And his name was Ronaldo.
He tried to score
But he missed
And it was poor.
Then next is was J-Lo
She was singing
Don't be fooled by the rocks I got
I'm still Jenny from the block.
She stopped singing
And a man called out
'She is winning.'
After that it was Girls Aloud
Singing *Underground*.
At 9.30pm at a party
People dancing up and down
To all the smash hit music
Then a person called Britney
Was dancing on stage
Singing and dancing
And having fun with her mates
And eating cakes.
This is the last one
Sean Paul is cool
When he's in a pool.
That's the end
Of my famous people poem.

Laura Walker (10)
South Borough Primary School

Dogs!

Dogs, dogs I love them, I have one myself,
He's cute, he's the best and in great health.
His breed's quite rare,
More than a house hare!

His name is Creed,
Do you know his breed?
I'm not making this up!
I've known him since a pup!

He's got a heart of gold,
He's very old,
As he goes into the sky,
I'll cry goodbye.

I don't want him to go,
I've been screaming the word, 'No!'
It's a very hard time,
It's such a crime.

But, may he rest in peace.

Emily Smith (10)
South Borough Primary School

Snow

Snow is falling all around
I watch it settle on the ground.

I can't wait to go out and play
I hope the snow will last all day.

It's soft and white but very nice
When it's night it will turn to ice.

When I see the last flake falling
I get a feeling about someone calling.

When it's gone I will feel so sad
I'll wait till next year which is not too bad.

Joanna Dillon (10)
South Borough Primary School

Creatures Of The Jungles

In jungle deep, it's early morning,
The mists are clearing, sun is dawning,
Tigers wake, stretching and yawning,
Ring tailed lemurs softly calling.

Deep in the outback, under noonday sun,
Ostriches tall, so fast when they run,
Koalas swing through trees having fun in the canopy,
Kookaburras laugh and shriek with glee.

It's teatime now, dusk comes around,
Foxes and badgers hunt on the ground,
Wild cats stalk their prey all round,
Wolves start to howl as the sun goes down.

Deepest oceans, dark as the night,
Dolphins and whales play in the light,
Sharks swim for their prey with all their might,
The sun is rising, what a beautiful sight.

Erin Anne Ross Elmer (9)
South Borough Primary School

Alliteration

One old orange on one oyster.
Two tiny tidy tigers.
Three thumping things thump thistles.
Four fish fly from Frankfurt.
Five frog fillets from France.
Six silly snakes slither sideways.
Seven stinky sausages slide singularly.
Eight emus eat elephant eggs.
Nine nectarines nibble nice nieces.
Ten tangerines tickle two turtles.
Eleven eels eat electric elephants.
Twelve twinkle twins twang twigs.

Philip Ellwood (11)
South Borough Primary School

Space Race

Once I had a race,
Going up to space.
First we had a look at Saturn,
But it looked like Manhattan!
Then we went to Mars
And we ate our chocolate bars!
Then we went through a foam cloud
But it looked like home.
After that, we went in our space truck,
I was thinking big bucks!
Then we went to Pluto,
I was thinking good-o!
Then we saw a gnome,
We were going home.
The gnome said the Earth was bust
Then we ripped the breadcrust.
I got a job but it was hard
To stay employed!

Jamie Potten (10)
South Borough Primary School

Snow

Snow is cold
Snow is so white
Snow is soft
Snow is crunchy
Snow is icy
Snow is very frosty
Snow is bumpy
Snow is flat
Snow is falling everywhere
Snow is fun!

Ellie Stevens (8)
South Borough Primary School

As I Grew Up!

Eighteenth of October was my special day
It was the day when my mother's big bump went away,
As I came out I cried, of course,
My mother still smiled even though she had used force.
One year passed and I was one year old,
I drew on the walls and I didn't do as I was told,
I had a big cot with an illustrated bunny,
I wore plump nappies, oh and my nose was always runny.
Then appeared the big bump again,
Mum had sore backs and yelled, *'Oh the pain!'*
As the baby was born they decided to call her Lily,
I got jealous of her and her socks that were frilly,
As I turned eight, I thought I looked cool,
But in my clippy-clops, I looked a right fool,
Now I'm ten and two years older
And at the moment I feel two years colder!

Rosie McGinn (10)
South Borough Primary School

Magic Snow

Why is snow so magic?
Why is it fun and filled with joy?
Why is snow fun to build with?
Why is snow crunchy and fun and squishy?
Why does snow make handprints and footprints?
You can make anything with snow because it is so magic.
Why does snow have to die when the sun comes up?
Why is snow so magic?

Adam Ross (8)
South Borough Primary School

Snow

Snow is on the ground,
I'm trying to make it round,
When I'm still in bed,
The kids are making the white snowman's head.

People are having blossom white snowball fights,
I think I'll go and join in,
Then all of a sudden, everyone stops
And they all look up, then suddenly down falls snow.

Everybody is screaming and shouting,
Then everyone builds bigger snowmen,
The soft snow is now six foot three
And that's much bigger than me,
Because I can't even see.

Giorgia Daniels (10)
South Borough Primary School

Snow

Snow soft as cloud fluff
Snowman's having some fun
Let's all join the fun
Snow is bright, snow is white
Making everybody happy
People giggling as loud as they can
Making mountains, making igloos
Making snowmen
Snow is flat, snow is icy
Snow is frosty
Snow is light when you pick it up
Everything shivering when it snows
It makes you freezing, it makes you cold
It makes you stiff, you can't move one bit.

Hibah Zubair (7)
South Borough Primary School

My Class

My teacher is very nice,
I wonder if she eats rice?
She is very smart
And has a big, warm heart.

Our helper is very kind,
She always asks me what's on my mind,
She also gives you advice,
But she hates all kinds of mice.

Our class is full of noise,
There is a boy mad about koi,
A boy is really, really smart,
All together we're one big, warm heart.

Rebecca Smy (10)
South Borough Primary School

Snow Time

The snow is white, it is fun
The snow melts in the sun.

When the snow falls the children come out to play
The children cry when it goes away.

The snow is flaky, the snow is small
The snow is different, the snow is cool.

When the snow is falling, the children dance around
When it stops falling, it's resting on the ground.

Walking in the winter snow
I never want it to go.

Hannah Reilly (9)
South Borough Primary School

Jump Or Jiggle

Kittens bounce
Dogs pounce.

Rabbits hop
Horses clop.

Snakes slide
Birds glide.

Kangaroos jump
Camels hump.

Frogs jiggle
Worms wiggle.

Rhinos charge
Hippos barge.

Lions walk
But I talk.

Ellie King (8)
South Borough Primary School

Motorbike

Motorbike, motorbike
Wheels burning
Engine working
Petrol heating
Mirrors shining
Motorbike, motorbike
Seat breaking
Crash helmet hurting
Brakes braking
Gears changing.

Leon Alcock (10)
South Borough Primary School

Bessy Bear

Bessy Bear
Everywhere.
On the weekend
Make new friends.
Friends are sad
Make them glad.
Time to play
Every day.
That makes you sad
Cheer up lad.
Play times are fun
For everyone.
Bessy Bear
Always there.
She's always there
When you need her.

Emma Whyatt (10)
South Borough Primary School

Spring

Spring, spring is almost here.
The green grass is very near.

Birds, birds in their nest.
No time for the parent to rest.

Flowers, flowers starting to grow.
The smell of them will be good, I know.

Lambs, lambs are playing everywhere.
The farmer will mind them with a lot of care.

Spring, spring is my favourite season.
I'll give you all no better reason.

Dean Wilson (10)
South Borough Primary School

My Puppy In Some Snow

My puppy got stuck in some snow but then he didn't come in.
I said, 'Charlie please come in,'
But then I thought I'd try once more but he still didn't come in.
I went out and looked but I couldn't see him.
'Oh no!' I said, he was stuck up a tree.
I got scared because it was very icy.
'How did you get up there Charlie?' I said.
He cried and cried and cried.
I know I thought to myself, *what about Dad's ladder?*
I got Dad's ladder but then I saw my cat Lucy stuck up there too.
Do you think Charlie chased Lucy up the tree?
I was really scared then.
How would I manage?
And then, Oh no, my rabbit had got stuck up the tree.
I was starting to get really scared.
How could I get them all down.
Oh no, my puppy's mum was also stuck up the tree.
The snow was now coming down again.
It made a long slide on the ladder.
Suddenly, one by one they came down.
First, Charlie, then Lucy, then Ellie, then my rabbit,
Finally my puppy's mum.
They were all safe at last.
They put footprints in the snow.
I could not lose them now
As I can follow their footprints.

Kirsty Samson (7)
South Borough Primary School

Snow

Snow is some cotton wool,
Laid about the place.

Snow is whipped cream,
Dropped on the floor.

Snow is white poster paint,
Slowly being wiped up.

Snow is shaving foam,
Sprayed by God up high.

Jessica McCafferty (10)
South Borough Primary School

Snowballs

S nowballs are cold
N obody is out to play
O nly a little snowman
W ho is all alone
B oys throw snowballs
A little girl having fun
L et's all play together
L ovely, lovely
S now.

Bethany Taylor (7)
South Borough Primary School

Bionic Cow

Mary had a bionic cow
It lived on safety pins
And every time she milked that cow
The milk came out in tins.

Ashleigh Maria Haines (10)
Wentworth Primary School

Footy Mad

I'm footy mad
I'm footy crazy
I'm footy all over
I support Liverpool
I own a swimming pool
I am very cool.

I'm footy mad
I'm footy crazy
I'm footy all over
I support Man U
And so should you
3-0 ha, ha, beat you.

I'm footy mad
I'm footy crazy
I'm footy all over
I support AC Milan
Because I can
And I am a man.

Brandon Lee (10)
Wentworth Primary School

In London Town . . .

In London town, they shot me down,
When I was just a lad,
I got a lot of injuries
And most of them were bad,
I only tried to break the bank
And nick a million quid,
But they shot me down and face it,
I was just a little kid!

Ben Crome (10)
Wentworth Primary School

Kids At School

There was a girl called Olly,
Who had a dolly named Molly,
So she took it to school and acted so cool
But that is the girl called Olly.

There was a girl called June,
Who always sung a nice tune,
So at her school she sung at the ball
And that is the girl called June.

There was a boy named Billy,
Who to Milly was quite mean,
So Milly wasn't quite keen to be seen,
With the boy named Billy.

There was a boy named Chris,
Who fancied two girls called Fliss and Bliss,
But Fliss he wanted to kiss,
So that was the boy named Chris.

Olivia Dove (9)
Wentworth Primary School

Nothing

If nobody ruled nobody
Nobody would know
No one could see anyone
Nowhere they could go
No one would walk up to no one
To look him in the eye
If nobody heard no voice
Nobody would reply.

Samantha Perry (11)
Wentworth Primary School

Fine Little Bunny Rabbit

Fine little bunny rabbit
Hopping in the field,
Saw a little boy
With a sword and shield!
'I am all mighty,
I am the one,
I am better than the moon
And even greater than the sun!'
He ran through walls,
He walked on water,
He killed his son
And even his own daughter.
'No!' screamed a voice coming from behind,
'You are turning evil, you are not very kind!'
The little bunny put down the sword and shield
And hopped back into the little bunny field!

Nicola Thomas (10)
Wentworth Primary School

God's Creation

God created a factory of which to produce a colourful land,
This land was made of sand,
His first attempt was to make a man,
But then he forgot a hand,
His next attempt was to make the land,
But he made the land a little bland,
His third attempt was to make the sea,
After that he made a tree.

After he made water, he attempted to make the ocean,
But all he ended up making was . . .
Commotion!

Abi Tait (11)
Wentworth Primary School

The Cat And The Kitten

There was a tiny kitten
In the little shed
Its mother had made her home there
About a month ago.

The kitten was very alert
When I went near
I gave them both some milk to drink
And made a little bed.

When I went back
To have another look
The kitten came out the door.

It seemed to know
I would be back
With a saucer of milk
Or more.

Kerry Mills (11)
Wentworth Primary School

What Is . . . The Sky?

The sky is a blue blanket, moving,
The sky is a sheet of pale, white paper,
With blue thumbprints all over it,
The sky is a sheet of pale, blue paper,
Blocking out the daytime sun,
The sky is a blue and black postage stamp,
Enlarged to fit the world,
The sky is a grey balloon,
Burst so blue, helium fills the world,
The sky is everything blue
And will always remain the same.

Elen Harris (11)
Wentworth Primary School

The World Of A Shoe!

The people wouldn't have been created,
Unless my shoe had broken.
It was a day that changed my life,
People were created and my shoe broke.

I never take my shoe off,
I never clean my feet,
I never cut my toenails,
I have very stinky feet!

They came out of my wart,
They made my feet itch,
They came out of my verruca,
My feet I had to ditch.

My shoe was getting small,
My shoe was getting cramped,
The people were growing tall,
My shoe was now getting very small.

Eventually my toenail,
Poked right through my shoe,
Oh no, but what could I do?

I went to the shops,
Immediately the people had already gone,
Created their world and singing their song.

They had their home,
I had my home,
We both lived happily ever after
And the world had begun.

Alice Palmer (10)
Wentworth Primary School

Creation Myth

The referee blew his whistle,
He blew his mighty whistle.
The great game began,
Yes, the greatest game began.
God, the manager,
God was the best manager
Of the angel team,
The wonderful angel team.
In the 90th minute,
The golden, 90th minute,
Michael made a pass,
A defender splitting pass.
Then Gabriel shot the ball,
Shot it with all his power.
It rolled into the net,
Rolled slowly into the net.
God's team had won the cup,
Won the cup forever.

After the game,
After the greatest game.
Their green ball was broken,
Broken very badly.
There were blue holes everywhere,
Blue holes everywhere.
Then God had an idea,
The greatest ever idea.
He said, 'Let us put people on this ball,
Thousands of them on this ball.
It will be turned into a world,
A new, amazing world.
They will be identical to us,
Identical to the greatest angels.
Then they can play football forever,
Until the end of time.'

The greatest ever idea.

Paul Moran (11)
Wentworth Primary School

School Poem

In class six,
There was a terrible mix,
With boys and girls
And strawberry swirls.

In class five,
There was a huge beehive,
Everywhere there were bees,
Sitting on boys' knees.

In class four,
A young girl got stuck in the door,
She need the loo,
But she had lost her shoe.

In class three,
A girl cut her knee,
There was blood everywhere,
Even in her hair.

In class two,
Samantha needed a poo!
She wanted to tell,
But she thought, *oh hell!*

In class one,
Charles broke his thumb,
He sat on a bench
And he smelt a big stench.

Michelle Martin (10)
Wentworth Primary School

School Days

It was time for Dickens group to read,
Half the group were acting like chickens.
The other half were acting bad
And Miss Anguish was very mad.

The first chapter was boring,
The rest of the class was roaring.
At last it was 10 to 12, saved by the bell,
RE was next, oh please, oh please, oh well.

Half-one what's new?
Oh no, not more school!
First the torture of the horrible stew,
Now I don't know what to do.

Three-fifteen, hooray, hooray, school's over,
Now I'm on my trip to Dover.
Over the hills, over the mountains,
Now we go out on our outings.

When we arrived, Mum made beef roast,
While Dad was telling us about the scary ghost.
But who cared? Not me,
All of a sudden I was stung by a bee.

The next day, time for school,
To my surprise the school had a pool,
Now I wonder if I like school.

Ben Hodges (11)
Wentworth Primary School

Her?

Where was she going?
Where is she now?
Back then it was snowing,
She was hot, she wiped her brow.

She knew that she was running,
Too fast to see things pass,
She had to use her cunning
While she slipped on dewy grass.

Were they going to get her?
What would they do?
Everything was such a blur!
Would she tell them what was true?

Soon they had found her,
Would they accept her plea?
What would next occur?
Who was she?

Katherine Joyce (11)
Wentworth Primary School

The Monster

M oody
O blivious
N octurnal
S hadowy
T empourous
E xperimental
R eigning
S wift.

Sean Middlemiss (10)
Wentworth Primary School

Gemma's First Birthday

Gemma, you're now one year old,
Your body's grown all big and bold.
Soon you'll be running, walking, talking, going to school,
Soon you'll be reading, writing, learning, growing up tall.
And we'll look back at photos of you when you were one,
Since you've had your first year under the sun.
But whether you're an author, a nurse or a vet,
We'll always know we could never get,
A girl as cute, lovely and as beautiful as you,
A little girl as special in our hearts as you . . .

Happy first birthday to my beautiful cousin,
Gemma!

Hayley Newman (11)
Wentworth Primary School

The Man From China

There was a man from China,
Who went to an American diner,
He ordered some chips,
He swallowed some pips
And had some injuries that were minor.

There was a boy called Billy,
Who woke up rather chilly,
He went for a jog,
Swallowed a frog
And had a squeaky voice that was silly.

Billy Cox (11)
Wentworth Primary School